CW01498090

HAVE YOU BEEN BLINDED?

FACING YOUR ASSUMPTIONS ABOUT GOD'S LEADERSHIP

SAMUEL WHITEFIELD

Have You Been Blinded? Facing Your Assumptions About God's Leadership
By Samuel Whitefield

Published by OneKing Publishing
PO Box 375
Grandview, MO 64030

Email: contact@oneking.global
Web: https://oneking.global

Dedicated to the Church—the people God is maturing to be His Son's companion

TABLE OF CONTENTS

INTRODUCTION

What if God is moving in the world in unprecedented ways but we are unable to see it because we have a spiritual blindness perpetuated by assumptions and wrong interpretations of Bible verses?

When crisis comes, it exposes our assumptions and reveals our faulty foundations. We live in a time when we face the pressure of small crises, but the Bible warns we are headed toward an unprecedented crisis—a disruption we cannot fully anticipate.

We are already experiencing great glory and great trouble, but this is only the beginning. The prophets were unable to adequately describe what is coming. In that day, every false assumption and weak foundation will be destroyed. We have a window to prepare for that crisis, but that window will not be open forever.

Wrong assumptions and fragile foundations can remain undetected for decades if we do not face what the Bible reveals about God, about ourselves, and about this age. We can be so confident in our assumptions that we do not seriously examine them according to the Scriptures, and this leads to spiritual blindness. And, when the day of crisis suddenly comes, we can suffer incredible loss. Before things intensify, we must address our spiritual blindness.

This challenge is not new. Some of Israel's best-known prophets succumbed to spiritual blindness because of their own assumptions. Their stories have been carefully preserved so we can be freed from our spiritual blindness, but we must be willing to examine our own lives in the light of their message.

Over two thousand years ago, a prophet filled with anxiety accused God of not answering his prayers and allowing calamity to go unchecked. God's first response to the prophet's accusation was a forceful, "Look, look! You cannot see what I'm doing."[1]

This prophet continued to argue with God, and God told him to write the entire argument down and send it everywhere. Their argument revealed a set of assumptions the prophet had made that had left him blind and unable to see what God was doing. Many of us hold the same assumptions, and like the prophet we are unaware we are blind. If we do not deal with our blindness, we will succumb to the same fear, confusion, and anxiety, and may even end up resisting what God is doing.

Spiritual blindness is especially challenging because we can be spiritually blind yet think we see. We can think we perceive or have insight into what God's purposes are in a given situation or time. When you are spiritually blind, you think you have insight into what God is doing, but in reality you cannot see what God is doing. We are heading into the most challenging days the earth has ever seen, and our blindness is a growing crisis that requires an urgent response.

People often accuse God of being uninvolved in the nations because they are blind.

God is much more active in the world than we imagine, but our assumptions about His ways are keeping us from seeing what He is doing. This is always dangerous, but in the days ahead things are going to escalate in ways we cannot currently anticipate. Right now, we are like a blind man walking toward a cliff. If we do not recover our sight, we will walk right off this cliff into an unforeseen catastrophe.

Spiritual blindness is difficult to resolve because you don't know you're blind— you think you can see. What if you have fallen prey to a spiritual blindness that leaves you unable to see what God is doing?

The good news is God wants to give us the ability to see. Jesus' well-known rebuke to the church in Laodicea urged them to address their blindness:

> *I counsel you to buy from me gold refined by fire, so that you may be rich, and white garments so that you may clothe yourself and the shame of your nakedness may not be seen, and salve to anoint your eyes, so that you may see. (Revelation 3:18)*

---

[1]Habakkuk 1:5.

We have more information about what is happening in our world than any other generation, and it is easy to become numb to the constant influx of information. If you live a relatively comfortable life, remember there are millions living in conditions you cannot imagine with little hope of deliverance. If you are a Christian, millions of your own *family* are presently caught in these crises.[2]

For example, there are currently millions of refugees in the earth who do not know if they will ever be able to go back to their homes or whether they will ever have a home again. Many parts of the world deal with the trauma of terrorism and political instability. Economic calamities threaten numerous nations. A single pandemic has shut down the world and completely reshaped its economy within a few weeks.

It is important not to minimize the pain and suffering presently in the world, but there is greater trouble looming on the horizon. Current events that dominate the news now are early "birth pains" of bigger things to come. If we do not face our fear, anxiety, assumptions, and accusations against God now, we will be unprepared for what lies ahead. We do not know when these disruptions will occur, but they are coming. For millions of people, they are already here.

It is easy to look at these events and feel hopeless, but if you let God heal your blindness, you will discover He is at work leading the nations in a surprising way.

A Familiar Crisis

Christians can identify many threats to their faith. They typically address things like immorality, compromise, cultural pressure, persecution, or complacency. However, most Christians have overlooked another threat to their faith. It's a threat many do not perceive but may be the greatest threat of all.

In the days ahead, the Church and the world will face a massive crisis. This crisis is not new. It has been with humanity for thousands of years, but very few are prepared for it. The disruptions we will face in the future are not the real crisis, but they will bring us face-to-face with the real crisis.

This crisis is the lack of a true knowledge of God—particularly when He leads history and our lives in ways we cannot comprehend.

---

[2]Hebrews 13:3.

A lot of what we assume we know about God is not true. We base it on faulty reasoning, wrong teaching, and unbiblical conclusions. Our knowledge of God is not robust enough for the days ahead, and much of what we assume to be true will be shattered. It may be shattered when your life goes in a direction you did not expect, or it may be shattered in a moment of turmoil.

God wants to expose the faulty foundations in our knowledge of Him now so He can heal us, and then our faith will not be shipwrecked in the coming days.

An Unsinkable Faith

About a hundred years ago, an "unsinkable" ship known as the *Titanic* began its maiden voyage across the Atlantic Ocean from England to New York City. It was well built, precisely engineered, and fully prepared for the journey. It was an enormous ship—much larger than ships had been up to that point. The ship was majestic with beautiful rooms and an impressive interior. The ship had been carefully designed to handle different kinds of accidents.

The *Titanic* sailed across the Atlantic with great confidence, but then the unthinkable happened. As the ship was sailing along one night, an iceberg suddenly came into view. The ship tried to avoid the iceberg but hit it instead. The ship's supposedly watertight compartments filled with water and quickly failed. Within hours, this majestic ship was on the ocean floor, and two-thirds of its passengers were dead.

The *Titanic* was an engineering marvel. It was well thought out and had groundbreaking technology designed to enable it to survive accidents that would sink other ships. It was the biggest and "safest" ship of its kind. When it faced an unexpected challenge, though, all the human effort that had gone into the ship came up short. An unperceived weakness was exposed, and design elements that had made the ship "unsinkable," ironically sealed the ship's fate once it struck the iceberg.

Like the *Titanic*, modern Christianity is impressive. We have done quite a bit of "engineering" in the Church. Much of it is good and has enabled the Church to steward resources for the advancement of the gospel. We should not despise or critique everything that has been accomplished. Much has been done at great cost out of love for Jesus, and many have benefited from it. But the Church is also currently headed toward a hidden iceberg.

This iceberg is not perceived by many, and if we do not see it and prepare for it now, the results will be catastrophic beyond anything we can imagine. Millions will fall away from the faith, and millions more will succumb to panic, anxiety, and fear. Around the world, many believers have already been forced to deal with this iceberg, but in the days ahead the entire Body will come face-to-face with it in a way that we cannot now imagine.

This "iceberg" is God Himself.

The Unexpected Conflict

A. W. Tozer famously identified the most important thing about a person:

> *What comes into our minds when we think about God is the most important thing about us. The history of mankind will probably show that no people has ever risen above its religion, and man's spiritual history will positively demonstrate that no religion has ever been greater than its idea of God. . . . For this reason the gravest question before the Church is always God Himself, and the most portentous fact about any man is not what he at a given time may say or do, but what he in his deep heart conceives God to be like.[3]*

We have developed ideas about God that are deeply entrenched in the minds of millions of Christians but are not true. These ideas seem reasonable to us, and we use Bible verses to defend them, but we have a knowledge of God according to our own thinking. Like the engineers of the *Titanic*, we have developed a "faith" that we think can survive every test, but we do not realize it cannot survive a "collision" with God.

Our view of God does not accommodate who God really is. Yet, God will not change who He is, nor is He ashamed of who He is. On the contrary, God is committed to shattering our false ideas about Him. He wants to be known in the earth *as He is*, and He is not concerned in the least about our opinions about who He is or what He should be. He has commissioned the Church to be the witness of who He is in

---

[3]A.W. Tozer, *The Knowledge of the Holy* (New York: HarperCollins, 1961), 1.

this age, and if our witness is not accurate, He is long-suffering, but the day will come when He reveals our false notions about Him that He might be known in truth.

Like the Titanic, *we are headed toward a collision with an "iceberg" we may not see.*

The Revelation of God

There are three times in this age God comes down visibly in the sight of His people to shift the way He deals with them. The first was the exodus, the second was the first coming of Jesus, and the third is the return of Jesus. Each time there is a new and unprecedented revelation of God. In the exodus, God revealed Himself to Israel as the Deliverer and the Bridegroom. In the first coming, God opened up a mystery by revealing Himself to us in a man.[4]

As John wrote, the second coming of Jesus is primarily about the *revelation* of who He is:

> *The revelation of Jesus Christ, which God gave him to show to his servants the things that must soon take place. . . . (Revelation 1:1)*

The return of Jesus is not primarily about the antichrist, suffering, or great calamities. It is primarily about the revelation of God in a way we have not yet known Him. We do not know when Jesus will return, but we must realize that God wants to be known, and the most dramatic events in history are designed to make Him known.

God wants us to know Him, but He wants to be known as He is and not as we think He is.

We are running out of time, but there is still enough left to avert this calamity if we will diligently give ourselves to the Word of God and allow the Holy Spirit to reveal God to us. The longer we delay this, the more serious our situation becomes. The *Titanic* sunk because the crew did not see the iceberg in time. They were sailing full speed in confidence in their assumptions about their condition. They had sailed across most of the Atlantic without any issues and were confident.

The further you go without examining your assumptions, the more confident you are in your own opinions. If we continue to sail with our present assumptions, we are headed for a fate like the *Titanic*'s, and it

---

[4] 2 Corinthians 4:4–6; Colossians 1:15; Hebrews 1:1–3.

will be too late when the "iceberg" of the knowledge of God appears unexpectedly. The good news is that God has plainly revealed Himself in Scripture and through His Son so we can know Him and have confidence in who He is. The problem is we have overlooked much of what God plainly says about Himself or created explanations that allow us to ignore what God plainly says.

There is only one way to remedy the problem—we must know God as He has revealed Himself, which will require us to radically alter the way we think about Him.

Many people believe the return of Jesus could come within a generation or two. While we do not know when He is coming, it easy to see that the season is shifting on the earth, and the world we are headed into is not the same world our ancestors lived in.

God is going to confront false ideas about Himself in ways we cannot currently imagine. He is not ashamed of who He is and how He has revealed Himself, even though much of what He says is not palatable to modern human thinking. God will challenge the Church *first*,[5] and if you do not allow the Bible to confront your thinking about God now, you may find yourself offended, fearful, or falling away from the faith in the days ahead. However, there is still time if we will allow Him to renew our thinking.

A Little Book That Reveals a Big God

Our journey will begin with a small book in the Old Testament called Habakkuk, which begins with an argument between God and a confused prophet. God's message to Habakkuk was so shocking that God told Habakkuk he would not have believed God's message if another prophet had brought it to him. God's conversation with Habakkuk is a critical key to recovering the knowledge of God. Before we look at that conversation, we need to rethink the way we approach God, and that is where we will start next.

We have to see the "iceberg" of who God is. As we enter this journey, many chapters will raise profound and painful questions that will not be answered until much later in the book. Do not give up on the journey. It will take us some time to identify the depth of our problem, but we will see the beauty of God's solution to our crisis.

---

[5] 1 Peter 4:17.

God designed the end of the age to confront the core human issue. Yet, very few people realize what the core human issue is. We tend to think it is the various sins or evil acts that we see around us. These are all serious, but they are not the core issue. They are *expressions* of the core issue. As we go, we will expose our core issue, and if we allow God to address it, we will be healed and discover a new intimacy with Him because we will know Him *as He is* and we will see Him *as He is*.

Let's go.

You Must See What You Have Not Seen

BIG QUESTIONS NEED ROBUST ANSWERS

Right now, many people look at the nations, and what they see fills them with anxiety and confusion. *What is going on? What does the future hold? Is there any solution? What is our answer to crisis and disruption in the earth?*

Even worse, many in the Church are also gripped by anxiety and confused even though the Church has God's answer to the crisis. Others in the Church have put their confidence in false hopes and wrong solutions, which are equally damaging.

The Bible predicts there will be a "people of understanding" who will give God's answers to these fears, anxieties, hopes, dreams, and uncertainties.[1] Are you a person of understanding? Do you want to be?

The Church and the nations are in desperate need of people with this understanding, which raises a profound question: *How do we become a people of understanding?*

We become a people of understanding by facing some of our deepest questions and God's answers to those questions. The process is painful, but it will transform us if we allow it to.

We have been given the gift of the Holy Spirit and the truth of the Word of God so we can become a people of understanding. The good news is that God does not hide the path to understanding. Though it is often avoided by us, He has made it clear. And for the record, you do not need to be a Bible scholar to become a person of understanding.

Understanding is not all about how much you know, but it is about how deeply you allow what you know to transform you.

The little, ancient book of Habakkuk contains profound answers to potentially painful questions like:

- Where is God?

---

[1] Daniel 11:33–35; 12:3.

- Why won't God answer my prayers?

- Why hasn't revival come?

- Does God not see and care about what is happening?

- Where is God in the midst of crisis?

- If God is good, why is there so much evil—and why does evil seem to prosper?

Humans have been asking these questions for thousands of years. Sadly, most of us are given shallow answers that use religious language but do not convey the knowledge of God. These answers are empty platitudes that offer little substantial comfort. Some may accept these superficial explanations while others end up cynical.

God is not silent, and the Bible contains real answers to these questions. God's answers will confront our perception of who He is with who He *really* is. We lack the knowledge of God when we never ask the difficult questions *or* we are unwilling to fully consider God's answers to those questions. We can try to avoid these questions, but there is a knowledge of God that does not come any other way.

Difficult questions expose us to new aspects of the knowledge of God, and if we do not ask these hard questions and allow the Bible's answers to transform us, we will lack a complete knowledge of God.

It is also possible to ask these questions but not hear God's answers. If you want a true knowledge of God, you must *ask* the hard questions and *submit* to God's answers. God's answers will bring comfort, but His answers will challenge, confront, and change us before they comfort us. His answers will confront some of your deepest assumptions and completely shift your paradigm of reality.

Habakkuk asked God hard questions, and God's response was so astonishing Habakkuk initially rejected God's answer. In His kindness, God firmly repeated His answer until Habakkuk was able to change his paradigm, and God will do the same thing for us through His Word.

In the pages ahead, we will be confronted by the Bible. You will probably be shocked by how God describes Himself. You will be forced to face things many Christians try to avoid. If you will stay the course and bear the tension, you will discover a deeper knowledge of God. You will find out there are things you thought were true that are not, and you will discover truth you would have never imagined. Above all, you are about to discover God in a way you have not known Him.

God is not shy. He has revealed Himself, and He wants us to know Him *as He is*. We will start with the prophet Habakkuk because his small book forces us to ask deep questions about who God is. His conversation with God is so significant that God instructed Habakkuk to write their conversation down carefully so it could be carried everywhere. Habakkuk's conversation with God will force you to ask some serious questions, but do not avoid the questions. Let them linger. Let them press you. These questions will lead you to discover the single root of all human sin, how God confronts that root, and His commitment to remove it.

If we want to know God, we must ask these hard questions and be willing to hear God's answers. God is not ashamed of His answers to our deepest questions, and He wants His Church to give those answers to the world. Sadly, in many cases, the Church is not the witness she is meant to be because she has not yet wrestled with God's answers to her deepest questions.

Our failure to grapple with what God has said is costing us a true knowledge of Him and preventing us from being a true witness.

When crisis comes, clichés that sound biblical will quickly fall apart because crisis reveals the depth of our faith. If our faith is shallow, a crisis will reveal it, but a shallow faith is just as deadly in a time of comfort as it is in a time of crisis. Right now, millions of Christians feel "OK," and they may be genuinely born again, but their knowledge of God is shallow. Their situation is far more precarious than they know. A person who is terminally ill but does not know it is no different from a terminally ill person who has received their diagnosis, and it is the same with our knowledge of God. We can be "sick" without feeling sick. We can be spiritually blind without knowing we're blind, but the sickness and the blindness still remain and cause damage.

We may feel "fine" while we are in desperate need of a true knowledge of God.

We *must* have a true knowledge of God. In the days ahead, millions will abandon the faith if they do not face the questions Habakkuk faced. Furthermore, the witness of the Church is at stake in how we answer these hard questions. God wants to give the earth a witness through His Church, but our witness often comes short of who God really is. In some cases, our witness is well-meaning but inaccurate.

Habakkuk's argument with God is a precious gift to us, enabling us to discover God as He is and become the witness God wants us to be. Let's jump into his story.

Blinded by Assumptions

Habakkuk was a prophet in ancient Judah who cared about his people and his nation. He was also a confident intercessor, convinced of God's purposes for God's people and his nation. Habakkuk lived in a time of disruption. Judah faced several internal issues. Injustice, immorality, idolatry, and other sins were increasing. It was clear Judah had abandoned her foundations. There were also external threats brewing.

The power base in the Middle East was rapidly shifting. The Assyrian Empire that had dominated the region had faded, and the Babylonian Empire was growing in strength. The borders in the region were changing quickly as well. Babylon was strong, proud, ambitious, and threatening. It was clear Judah was headed for a confrontation with Babylon. Though Judah had serious issues, the temple in Jerusalem was still standing, so Habakkuk and others had complete confidence God would protect Judah and judge "wicked" Babylon.

These challenges fueled Habakkuk's intercession. He kept praying, convinced he knew what God would do. He also used Bible verses to back up his convictions. From everything we know, he was a faithful follower of YHWH, a prophet, and an intercessor concerned about the issues his people were facing. He appeared to be the perfect description of a faithful remnant.

This is what makes his book so shocking.

There were no obvious flaws in Habakkuk, and yet he did not see God answering his prayers. As the geopolitical situation deteriorated, anxiety and fear took root in Habakkuk's heart. *Where is God? Why won't He answer?* Fueled by anxiety and assumptions, Habakkuk made a bold complaint against God and accused God of not being faithful to respond.

God responded with strength. He did not expose any hidden sin in Habakkuk. Instead, He exposed something bigger—something deeper. Habakkuk had assumptions about Bible verses, his nation, and God.

Even though Habakkuk was a member of the "faithful remnant," his assumptions were profoundly wrong.

God directly confronted Habakkuk's paradigm of reality. God's response was so shocking, Habakkuk rebuked God and repeated his complaint. Habakkuk's response exposed how tightly he held to his convictions. These were convictions he believed came from Scripture, but he did not realize they were formed by cultural assumptions. Habakkuk genuinely loved God, but he had become blinded by his assumptions. When God suddenly exposed his blindness, Habakkuk could not grasp what he was hearing.

Habakkuk had not only misinterpreted what God was doing, he had made assumptions about God. Those assumptions *seemed* biblical, but in fact they had made him blind and unable to see. Habakkuk had to discover who God really was. He was not like Habakkuk thought He was.

God instructed Habakkuk to write down their confrontation so it could be easily read and spread everywhere. The reason is simple: Habakkuk's blindness is *our* blindness. Like Habakkuk, we have certain assumptions about God and reality that are not true. We may use Bible verses to support those assumptions. We may have learned them at church. They may be deeply held and culturally familiar. But that doesn't change the fact that these assumptions are false.

Our assumptions will ultimately make us blind. We will become unable to see what God is doing, intercede without understanding, and become vulnerable to anxiety and fear when reality does not align with our assumptions. Most tragic of all, we will develop an understanding of God that is deficient at best and idolatrous at worse because our assumptions influence our concept of who God is.

When our assumptions are confronted, we usually resist the confrontation like Habakkuk. We use Bible verses out of context. We pull on convictions shaped more by our culture and human intuition than the knowledge of God, but we are convinced we know God. We listen to leaders who affirm our assumptions and reject those who challenge them. We are quick to interpret events and give "prophetic opinions" of what God is doing while completely unaware that we are blind.

Blinded by Confidence

Our assumptions are shaped by our culture, our human wisdom, our influences, our experiences, and our interpretation of the Bible. When we do not recognize these assumptions and refuse to change them when they are exposed, they become strongholds in our minds. The longer we refuse to change, the more dire the situation becomes as we grow in confidence in ideas that feel right but are not true.

Over time, we become confident in our blindness if it is not addressed.

Spiritual blindness is especially challenging. A man who is physically blind knows he is blind because he cannot see and depends on others to describe reality to him. He cannot see what is actually there and knows he needs insight, but spiritual blindness does not work this way. Spiritual blindness is not the inability to see. It is a condition where you see *through a human lens all the while assuming it is God's lens.*

When you are spiritually blind, you interpret history and reality through a human lens that may be informed by Bible verses, and you assume that is how God sees reality. It seems reasonable to humans, but God calls this *blindness* because humans are born blind, spiritually speaking. We must let God reveal reality and truth to us. When we use our understanding to form our opinions of God, ethics, reality, history, and culture, we are blind because what is true must be revealed by God.

When we think about spiritual blindness, we automatically assume this only applies to people caught in some deep deception or those who reject and deny the Scripture. Spiritual blindness can be very subtle, though. It can also be partial. A person can be genuinely saved and yet unable to see. This is why Habakkuk's story is so important. He was "saved." He was a part of the faithful remnant doing all the right things, and yet he had blindness. If it could affect Habakkuk, it can affect us. If you do not believe blindness can affect you, you are already at risk.

What if you have assumptions about God that are profoundly wrong? What if you cannot accurately see what He is doing in history? What if you view reality through a distorted lens? What if you have used Bible verses to support assumptions that keep you from a true knowledge of God?

Crisis has a way of exposing our blindness. In Habakkuk's case, a geopolitical threat exposed his blindness. It could be a personal crisis, a family crisis, or a national crisis. But when crisis confronts us, we generally respond in one of three ways:

1. We painfully allow God to redefine our understanding of who He is.

2. We walk away from the faith disillusioned when we discover God is different from the way we had imagined Him to be.

3. We strengthen ourselves in our blindness which sets us up to suffer great loss and miss what God is doing while we remain confident in a hope that is not real.

The Bible is a gift that allows us to confront our blindness before our blindness is exposed by a crisis. However, we have to let the Bible reveal God to us in His own words. We cannot read it through our own lens or add our own explanations. We cannot resolve certain tensions. If we will allow God to confront us through what is written about Him in His Word, we can have our blindness healed before the crisis.

We have to let the Bible shape us, but instead we often try to shape the Bible.

We must let God reveal to us who He is even if that disrupts everything we think is true about reality and forces us to dismantle some of our core convictions about life, God, history, and humanity. If we will not ask this question now, we will be forced to ask it in a day of crisis, and there is no guarantee we will respond correctly amid the crisis. Furthermore, the Bible warns us this age will end with a crisis far beyond any other crisis—a crisis not even comparable to Habakkuk's crisis.[2] This should put an urgency in our hearts to have a true knowledge of God that can endure the most difficult hour of history.

Habakkuk is a biblical tool that enables us to confront our blindness before a day of crisis. It will lead us into the knowledge of God if we allow it to.

Are you ready to confront your blindness? It's not easy. Many cannot stand the tension of realizing they have profound convictions about God and reality that are in fact not true, so they quickly find an explanation that lets them escape the confrontation. Life-saving surgery is always an invasive and painful process, but it is necessary. Spiritual surgery is no different.

It's time to let God define our reality through His Word.

---

[2]Jeremiah 30:7; Daniel 12:1; Joel 2:2; Matthew 24:21.

A Bold Complaint

Many believers subconsciously assume God was more involved in the nations in the days of the Old Testament, but this is not biblical. God is just as involved in the nations now as He was in the Old Testament. He still raises up kings and tears them down even in a time of widespread democracy.[1] God has not surrendered His sovereignty over the nations, nor is He silent.

The only difference between our time and the ancient world is that we have prophetic commentary in the Old Testament that gives us insight into God's activity in the prophets' time. This prophetic commentary was necessary because the ancient Israelites did not recognize God's work in the nations. Like us, their nationalism and their assumptions about God often kept them from perceiving His activity or responding to it.

This prophetic commentary has been given to us so we will know God's ways and be thoroughly convinced He is leading history in our time.

Habakkuk tells the story of a confrontation between Habakkuk and God. Habakkuk's fears and anxiety had led him to pray desperately, but his prayers seemed to go unanswered, so he accused the Lord of being uninvolved and uncaring. He could not have been more wrong.

Habakkuk was concerned God was overlooking his nation's crisis, but he never imagined God was more intricately involved than he thought.

Habakkuk had many assumptions about what God should do, and he made a bold complaint when God did not act according to his expectations. God answered his accusations and told Habakkuk to

---

[1]Daniel 2:21, 37–38; Isaiah 45:1; Romans 13:1.

write down their conversation in plain language so it could be carried everywhere.[2]

Habakkuk had an incomplete knowledge of God that kept him from seeing what God was doing in his generation.

God warned Habakkuk that his nationalistic assumptions had blinded him. Habakkuk and his people, like the people on the *Titanic*, were headed for an "iceberg" that would ultimately sink their nation, but they could not see it. This "iceberg" was the looming invasion of Babylon. God was deeply involved in the situation, but Habakkuk's knowledge of God was not robust enough to find God in the situation. The prophet was blinded by his assumptions.

Like the ancient Israelites, we often cannot perceive God's ways due to our own assumptions about Him. We are also blinded by our assumptions.

We must learn Habakkuk's lesson to know God as He is *and* to perceive what He is doing in our generation. Often, we can see God's work in hindsight, and we may even anticipate what God will do in the future, but we must become a people who can see God at work in the present.

Habakkuk's complaint was not unique to Habakkuk. If we want a true knowledge of God, we must allow God to confront us as He confronted Habakkuk. Habakkuk was blinded by his nationalism, and his convictions about God were so strong that he rebuked God when God answered his complaint. Like Habakkuk, we also hold certain assumptions that cause us to resist God.

God wanted His response to Habakkuk recorded because it is a response to *our* accusations and *our* assumptions.

Habakkuk's encounter warns us that some of our deepest desires and loudest prayers could be focused on something opposite to what God is doing. Habakkuk repented, but thousands of Israelites perished because they did not. If we do not deal with our blindspots, we will not perceive God's work in our generation, we will develop a distorted view of who God is, and we will take offense with His leadership.

The good news is that God addressed Habakkuk's blindness and set him free. He will do the same for us if we will listen and let Him.

---

[2]Habakkuk 2:2.

Habakkuk's Crisis

The book of Habakkuk opens with Habakkuk's pain over Judah's crisis during the seventh century BC. Under the reign of King Josiah, Israel had experienced a season of revival, but time revealed the people's devotion to God was only superficial. Habakkuk was grieved by Judah's compromise, and prophets had warned trouble was coming.

Assyria conquered and destroyed the Northern Kingdom of Israel, but God miraculously delivered Judah from Assyria.[3] The relief was temporary, however, because a more powerful threat emerged. Babylon conquered Assyria and quickly became the strongest empire in the region under Nebuchadnezzar's leadership. When Habakkuk wrote his book, Babylon was already a very serious threat to Judah's sovereignty.

Unless God delivered Judah, she would not survive the expansion of the Babylonian Empire. God had delivered Judah from Assyria, but there was an eerie prophetic silence in the land regarding deliverance from Babylon.

The Frustrated Intercessor

The looming Babylonian threat drove Habakkuk to intercession:

> *Lord, how long shall I cry for help, and you will not hear? Or cry to you "Violence!" and you will not save? Why do you make me see iniquity, and why do you idly look at wrong? Destruction and violence are before me; strife and contention arise. So the law is paralyzed, and justice never goes forth. For the wicked surround the righteous; so justice goes forth perverted. (Habakkuk 1:2–4)*

You can feel Habakkuk's fear and anxiety. Babylon was strong and ambitious. Habakkuk knew a confrontation between Judah and Babylon would be violent, and the odds were not in Judah's favor. Babylon had already rewritten several national boundaries, and Habakkuk was afraid Judah would be next.

Habakkuk's first complaint is a familiar complaint:

> *How long shall I cry for help and you not hear? Or cry to you . . . and you will not save?*

---

[3] 2 Chronicles 32:20–22; Isaiah 37:36–38.

Habakkuk was frustrated, confused, and discouraged because his intercession did not seem to be working. He had been praying and waiting for God's response, but the expected response had not come. It seemed like God was not even listening. What else could he do?

Habakkuk had prayed passionately, but the crisis had only escalated. There is an obvious pain in his voice as he asks, *"How long do I have to keep praying? How long will you ignore me?"* Habakkuk needed God to act and act soon, or the Babylonian invasion would no longer be a threat; it would be a reality.

Habakkuk was a frustrated intercessor.

Habakkuk kept praying, and the Babylonian threat kept growing, so he began to panic. In frustration, Habakkuk responded to God's silence with several complaints.

Habakkuk's First Major Complaint: God Was Not Listening

Habakkuk expressed a common complaint: *We have prayed, but God has not answered.* His complaint is easy to identity with if you have prayed for something for years and decades and there seems to be little change:

> *O LORD, how long shall I cry for help, and you will not hear? Or cry to you "Violence!" and you will not save? (Habakkuk 1:2)*

Habakkuk complained about God's silence and expressed his frustration over God's failure to act. He had cried out, *"Violence!"* to remind God that Israel was facing an imminent crisis from a Babylonian invasion. You can almost hear Habakkuk scream, *"Do You not see what is going on down here?!"* Habakkuk had a very clear expectation that God would respond, but God had not saved His people. The formula was not working.

Habakkuk's Second Major Complaint: God Will Not Save

Habakkuk issued his second major complaint in verse 3:

> *Why do you make me see iniquity, and why do you idly look at wrong? Destruction and violence are before me; strife and contention arise.*

Habakkuk turned his focus from the Babylonian threat to Israel's internal crisis. Habakkuk saw "wrong" (ESV) and "wickedness" (NASB95) but little hope for revival in the nation. Habakkuk implied the condition of the nation was God's fault because God was looking "idly" at wrong instead of sending revival. Habakkuk had prayed, but God had not answered Habakkuk's prayers with revival, so he blamed God for the iniquity and trouble he saw. If God really wanted to stop the growth of sin, He could, and His failure to respond to Habakkuk's prayer was empowering wickedness.

Habakkuk was in a crisis of faith. Why wasn't God saving the nation?

The sin in the nation was causing breakdowns in society. People were embracing lawlessness. The leadership of the nation was corrupt, and unjust laws allowed people to take advantage of each other:

Destruction and violence are before me; strife and contention arise. (v. 3)

You can feel panic in Habakkuk's voice. Habakkuk knew what had happened to the northern tribes of Israel. They had turned from God, become proud, tolerated injustice, and rejected the prophets' warnings of military invasion. When Assyria threatened the Northern Kingdom, Israel tried to survive through her military strength and alliances with other nations, but it did not work. The Assyrians, a brutal and terrible people, conquered Israel and carried thousands into captivity.

Judah believed God would not allow Babylon to conquer Jerusalem because of the temple, but Habakkuk recognized Judah was following the pattern of northern Israel. He was beginning to panic because the nation was deep in sin, and a conflict with Babylon was becoming inevitable. God seemed silent, and Habakkuk was not convinced his compromised nation could survive a confrontation with the strength and violence of Babylon. The prayer for revival was genuine, but it was also an attempt to avoid a military crisis. Habakkuk had very real concerns God would not protect the nation from Babylon because of Judah's sin.

The leadership of the nation was breaking down, and the people were divided by their opinions. There was no unified repentance as the strife and contention grew.

The threat of crisis can unify a people, or it can also expose their true condition. In this case, the increasing injustice in Israel's society and the looming military threat exposed their deep division and disagreement.

Despite all these issues, the nation was confident they would find an escape from the mounting crisis. The king was confident he could navigate regional politics and secure alliances to protect the nation. The people still believed the army could protect the city. Everyone assumed God would ultimately protect the city because His temple was there. False prophets assured the people of YHWH's continuing protection and predicted a season of peace and blessing. It was inconceivable that God would let the only temple to the one true God be destroyed by a pagan invader. Judah *had* to survive so God could have a temple and a witness in Jerusalem.

The entire nation was blinded by nationalism mixed with religious presumption.

Habakkuk's Third Major Complaint: God's Word Is Paralyzed

Habakkuk gave his final complaint in verse 4:

> *So the law is paralyzed, and justice never goes forth. For the wicked surround the righteous; so justice goes forth perverted.*

Habakkuk lamented the law was "paralyzed" and powerless over the hearts and minds of the people. Habakkuk remembered the days of Josiah when he had rediscovered the law and the nation had experienced a brief revival. For a moment, it looked like the nation would return to the Word of God, but now God's law seemed "paralyzed" as the people openly disregarded His commands. Their disregard of the law was a manifestation of the real issue: *The nation had lost the fear of the Lord.*

Because the nation no longer feared the Lord, justice did not go forward. The powerful in the nation abused their leadership and took advantage of the weak and the poor because they did not fear the Lord.

Blinded by Nationalism

Though Habakkuk recognized Judah's sin, when he compared Judah to Babylon, he automatically categorized Babylon as "wicked" and Israel as "righteous." Habakkuk was blinded by his nationalism and his assumption that Judah was "bad" but "not as bad" as Babylon; therefore, he accused God of being unjust because God had not answered Habakkuk's prayer and eliminated the Babylonian threat.

Like Habakkuk, we tend to evaluate nations and assume God agrees with us.

Habakkuk's final complaint was bold. Because God had not answered his prayer, justice was perverted. Habakkuk assumed God was committed to Judah's safety and prosperity, and he expected revival to solve the issues of injustice, end idolatry, strengthen the economy, and bring political security. Habakkuk recognized Judah's sin, but his nationalism convinced him it would be unjust for Babylon to conquer Judah.

Habakkuk did not realize that he was committed to something God was not committed to.

Summarizing Habakkuk's Complaint

To grasp Habakkuk's message, we must understand he was in pain over unanswered prayer. As I've mentioned before, we can sense the fear in Habakkuk's voice. The future looked grim. Habakkuk's chief complaint was that God had not responded to his prayer, and because God is sovereign over the nations, God's inactivity effectively amounted to His promotion of wickedness and darkness.

Habakkuk had prayed, fasted, and repented, and yet things did not seem to be improving. He had done everything he knew to do, but God had not done His part. Habakkuk was exhausted, burdened, and emotionally ragged over the condition of his nation while God did not seem to be concerned. Despair closed in on Habakkuk, and he finally broke and challenged God with the complaint that God was uncaring, unmoved, and uninvolved.

Would God ever see or act? Did God truly care? If God would respond to Habakkuk, things would be radically different.

A Modern Version of an Ancient Complaint

The fear that Habakkuk felt when he looked across the Middle East is a common fear. Millions also feel anxiety when they consider economic challenges, political instability, terrorism, war, pandemics, and other disruptions. Like Habakkuk, many have also prayed, but it does not seem to be "working." Few will verbalize it, but many wonder, *Why is God silent? Does He not care about what is going on down here?*

Habakkuk's complaint centered on one issue: He had prayed, and God was not responding to his intercession.

Habakkuk's complaint is especially relevant to our generation because there has been a dramatic increase in prayer over the last several decades. Even young adults have a growing interest in prayer. New expressions of prayer have emerged from fresh prayer movements. Many nations have hosted large stadium gatherings of prayer. Many cities have "houses of prayer" that host extended hours of prayer, and some cities even have prayer meetings that go 24/7. Churches are also searching for new rhythms of prayer.

There has never been as much prayer in the earth as there is now.

Prayer has been growing for decades—going at least back to the 1950s and the modern Korean prayer movement—and we can see God's hand moving on His Church. Much of the increase in prayer has been driven by the threat of crisis, just as it was with Habakkuk. Millions have turned to prayer, hoping to avert and solve crises, but we have seen an increase in disruption and have not seen the revival millions have prayed for. The longer this continues, the easier it becomes to wonder if God really hears our prayers and, if so, does He care?

When we pray and do not see the desired outcome, it significantly affects our emotions. We can easily become disillusioned, just like Habakkuk, and disillusionment easily leads to anxiety, fear, and accusations.

There are more people praying for a move of God than at any other time in history, but sin still abounds, and there seems to be no end to injustice. Not only do we face serious moral issues, we face worldwide uncertainty. There are more refugees than at any point in history. Freedom and human rights are threatened in many nations. Some nations have descended into division and sectarianism with no hope of unity. Political instability has become the norm. Pandemics can alter every area of life in a moment.

Many believers have prayed for years, but their nations seem in worse condition than when they began praying. After decades of prayer, discouragement can kick in. Accusations can rise: "Where is God? Why isn't prayer working? Why does God seem silent and unmoved by our plight?"

Habakkuk's complaint represents the way many believers feel, and if we do not answer this complaint biblically, millions of believers will become bitter and offended at a God they think does not answer prayer.

Modern Struggles with Ancient Problems

Ancient Judah's hopes are our hopes, and Judah's struggles are our struggles. We will see in a moment that Habakkuk's assumptions are also our assumptions. Even more troubling, many of our preachers give messages that are remarkably similar to the messages carried by Judah's false prophets.

Like Habakkuk, we are burdened by the sins we see in society, but we also compare ourselves to other people and assume other people are *more wicked*. We agree our people may deserve discipline, but think "other people" deserve judgment. We assume God is fully committed to our nation's success and His plan will include national revival, economic prosperity, peace, and international prominence.

We categorize sin in degrees. We assume that some nations need destruction because of their sin while other nations merely need rehabilitation. We automatically assume that it would be an *injustice* for some nations to be threatened by other "more wicked" nations. Like Habakkuk, we carry deep assumptions because we look at the world through a lens partially informed by the Bible yet deeply shaped by our culture.

Many have "tried prayer" with very specific expectations about how God will answer, but those answers have not come. The increasing groan in the Church is growing louder: "God, we have prayed and prayed, but where is revival? Why is our nation not saved? Do You even hear us? What's the use of prayer?"

God was kind enough to answer Habakkuk, and His answer shattered Habakkuk's worldview. God's answer to Habakkuk is His answer to us, and that is where we will turn next.

YOU MUST SEE WHAT YOU HAVE NOT SEEN

We do not know how long Habakkuk searched for an answer to his complaint. No doubt he uttered his complaint many times, praying, waiting, longing, and hoping for a reply. Then, one day, God suddenly spoke:

> *Look among the nations, and see; wonder and be astounded. For I am doing a work in your days that you would not believe if told. (Habakkuk 1:5)*

Many translations put an exclamation point at the end of the first sentence to show the strength of the Lord's reply. Habakkuk's accusations were bold and passionate, and now it was the Lord's turn to challenge Habakkuk. The Lord's response began with a firm command: *Look!*

The first thing the Lord commanded Habakkuk to do was to "look" among the nations—to see something Habakkuk had not seen.

The implication was obvious: Habakkuk had accused the Lord of being absent, uncaring, and uninvolved because he had not seen what God was doing. Habakkuk's assumptions and expectations had blinded him. When God did not do what Habakkuk expected, Habakkuk accused God of being unresponsive and aloof, but he was about to find out he could not be more wrong.

Habakkuk's inability to see is at the heart of his book.

Habakkuk introduced the book as the message that he "saw":

> *The oracle that Habakkuk the prophet saw. (Habakkuk 1:1)*

Throughout the book, the subject of seeing or vision comes up repeatedly because that is the actual issue.[1] Habakkuk thought he saw what God was (or was not) doing, but he did not. He wrote the book this way so we would face the same issue. We think we see, but like Habakkuk we probably do not really see.

God commanded Habakkuk to "look among the nations" because his fixation on Judah's immediate success had obscured his view of God's larger plan. Habakkuk assumed he knew God's agenda, but his political hopes and fears had kept him from seeing what God was doing. Habakkuk's chief complaint was that God was not involved, but God was involved—much more involved than Habakkuk had imagined.

Habakkuk had confidence in his perspective, but he needed to "look" again. This time he needed to look "and see." God was saying, "Habakkuk, what do you see? Look beyond Judah to My larger work. Look again, what do you see?"

God commanded Habakkuk to look and be *astounded.* Translations often use two words here, but in the original Hebrew, God repeated the same word twice (תמה). He literally told Habakkuk "be astounded, astounded." Repeating the same word twice was a way of emphasizing the word, and it shows the word was spoken with force and intensity. It is the same as what we do when we put a word in bold or add an exclamation point. Habakkuk was commanded *be astounded!*

The root meaning of the word God used is "be astounded, dumbfounded, and bewildered."[2] God was confronting Habakkuk's confident complaint. God's answer was going to *astonish* Habakkuk. God's initial answer would terrify Habakkuk and confront Habakkuk's assumptions about how God fulfills His purposes for the nations. God was going to shatter Habakkuk's paradigm and expose his inability to perceive what God was doing in his generation. God was about to give Habakkuk an answer to his complaint, but God warned Habakkuk he would not comprehend the answer. God wanted to break Habakkuk's confidence in his own wisdom.

---

[1] Habakkuk 1:1, 3, 5, 13; 2:1–3; 3:6–7, 10.

[2] Ronald F. Youngblood, "2518 תָּמַהּ," ed. R. Laird Harris, Gleason L. Archer Jr., and Bruce K. Waltke, *Theological Wordbook of the Old Testament* (Chicago: Moody Press, 1999), 972.

You Would Not Believe What I Am Doing

Habakkuk's accusations had revealed his view of God, so God directly addressed Habakkuk's complaint that He was aloof, inactive, and uninvolved:

> *I am doing a work in your days that you would not believe if told. (Habakkuk 1:5)*

Habakkuk had accused God of doing nothing, but in reality God was very active. You can almost hear God say, "Habakkuk, I've been very busy." Not only was God at work, God warned Habakkuk His work was so astounding that Habakkuk would not believe it if someone else told him.

Furthermore, the "you" in this verse is plural and not singular. God's response to Habakkuk was directed to the entire nation because Habakkuk's blindness and his complaint reflected a corporate problem. As a prophetic man, Habakkuk needed to see what others did not see, but he had become blind because he had adopted the nation's assumptions. God wanted to address His people through the message to Habakkuk, and He wants to address us through His words to Habakkuk.

God was saying, "Habakkuk, I am about to tell you what I am doing. However, if Jeremiah or any of My other prophets gave you this message, you would not believe them. You would rebuke any person who brought you this message just as you have complained against Me. Without the force of My voice and the weight of My presence, you would dismiss what you are about to hear."

God's warning shows how profound Habakkuk's assumptions were. He was so confident in his ideas that, even if another prophet revealed what God was doing, Habakkuk would have had more confidence in his understanding than in the word of the Lord. This statement was unsettling but true. Habakkuk's first response to the Lord would reveal just how confident he was in his assumptions.

What was God about to say that Habakkuk would refuse to hear from any other messenger? The answer came immediately:

> *"For behold, I am raising up the Chaldeans, that bitter and hasty nation, who march through the breadth of the earth, to seize dwellings not their own." (Habakkuk 1:6)*

God began His reply with "behold." The Hebrew word (הִנֵּה) is an interjection that demands attention. It means "Look! See!"[3] It was a command to Habakkuk to open his eyes to recognize what God was doing. We use interjections to express emotion at the beginning of a sentence, so you must feel God's emotions in His response to Habakkuk. Habakkuk cannot see, but God wants Him to see. He's trying to open Habakkuk's eyes by commanding him to *look!* God's repeated command to look reveals the true crisis: *Habakkuk is an intercessor, and he is a prophet, but he cannot see. He lacks prophetic insight. His internal assumptions have kept him from seeing what God is doing.*

God followed the command to look with a stance that made Habakkuk's mind explode, his emotions overflow, and his body tremble: *"I am raising up the Chaldeans."* It is impossible for us to fully grasp how shocking this statement was to Habakkuk. The Babylonians (Chaldeans) were the people Habakkuk was the most terrified of. They were an ambitious, powerful, pagan nation ready to conquer Judah. The growing Babylonian threat had driven Habakkuk to intercession and provoked his complaint that God was not doing anything. Now, God was emphatically taking credit for the very thing Habakkuk had prayed against.

Habakkuk had been praying, hoping to stop something God was doing in his generation.

Habakkuk had probably prayed against this threat for years. He had begged God to "intervene" in the situation. The answer had finally come, but it was impossible to comprehend: God was taking credit for the advance of a pagan nation against Habakkuk's people. No wonder God warned Habakkuk that he would not believe this message if it came from another prophet.

God's assault on Habakkuk's wisdom did not stop.

God described the Babylonians precisely to make the message clear to Habakkuk. God called them a "bitter and hasty nation." The NIV better captures the meaning of this phrase by describing Babylon as a "ruthless and impetuous people."

---

[3]Carl Philip Weber, "510 הן," ed. R. Laird Harris, Gleason L. Archer Jr., and Bruce K. Waltke, *Theological Wordbook of the Old Testament* (Chicago: Moody Press, 1999), 220.

God knew precisely who the Babylonians were, and He took credit for their success.

A Nightmare Come True

In verses 7–11, God continued to describe the nature of Babylon:

They are dreaded and fearsome; their justice and dignity go forth from themselves. Their horses are swifter than leopards, more fierce than the evening wolves; their horsemen press proudly on. Their horsemen come from afar; they fly like an eagle swift to devour. They all come for violence, all their faces forward. They gather captives like sand. At kings they scoff, and at rulers they laugh. They laugh at every fortress, for they pile up earth and take it. Then they sweep by like the wind and go on, guilty men, whose own might is their god!

God was fully aware of the character of the Babylonians, and He took credit for their rise to regional prominence. God affirmed Habakkuk's worst fears by predicting Babylon would march through the earth and possess dwelling places that were not theirs. They would conquer nations through their brutality, and this would include Judah. They were "hasty," meaning they would make rash decisions in their aggression toward other peoples. They were swift, wicked, and arrogant. They would not respect kings, armies, or God's law. They were going to set up siege mounds, conquer strongholds, and gather captives like the sand. They would be arrogant and massively successful for a time.

It was exactly what Habakkuk feared most, and he never imagined God would be involved in his worst nightmare.

God wanted Habakkuk to *look* and see the aspects of His glory that are revealed in judgment.[4] Habakkuk was looking for God's glory in patient mercy, but God's glory is also seen in His judgments.

Who Will Believe Our Report?

As we will see, Habakkuk could not initially accept the answer he received. Habakkuk could not believe God was using Babylon's success and Judah's failure to advance His purposes. He could not fathom the logic of it all, and his confusion is a troubling warning to us.

---

[4]Psalm 9:16; 48:11; 50:11; 96; 98; Isaiah 26:9.

The people of Israel and the prophets of old frequently could not grasp what God was doing in their time, and yet we confidently claim to know exactly what God is doing in our time.

Habakkuk's confusion was not an isolated event. When Isaiah prophesied the mystery of the coming Deliverer, he predicted people would find God's plan impossible to believe:

Who has believed what he has heard from us? And to whom has the arm of the LORD been revealed? (Isaiah 53:1)

This prophecy was a prediction of Jesus' humiliation, suffering, and death. Not only did Isaiah's generation not believe his prophecy, many who saw the prophecy fulfilled did not believe it either. Many found it impossible to believe this crucified Man could be the Divine Human and the long-awaited Messiah. Even though He had unusual power, rose from the dead, and ascended into heaven, many did not believe because their expectations were already formed, and Jesus did not match what they were looking for.

We can be blind to what God is doing in the earth because of our presuppositions of how His plan will come to pass.

Two thousand years after the crucifixion, we have forgotten just how shocking it was. God's work has been surprising throughout history, and the crucifixion was not the first time God bewildered His people with His leadership. God confronted Isaiah, Habakkuk, and ancient Israel with His leadership of history.

What if God confronts our expectations?

For example, many have very detailed conclusions about the events that surround Jesus' return and strong convictions that we will not be surprised, shaken, or offended by what God does, but God has repeatedly surprised His people with His leadership. If we do not learn this lesson, we may find our hearts vulnerable to offense when God accomplishes His purposes in unexpected ways.

The gift of the Holy Spirit can bring us into agreement with God, but that does not mean He will not surprise us in ways we cannot imagine.

The return of Jesus is the most visibly dramatic event[5] in history, and it will bring unprecedented disruption. It will include the end of

---

[5] I use the phrase, "visibly dramatic," because the cross is by far the most shocking thing God has done.

this age, the judgment of evil, the resurrection of the dead, the return of God to the planet, and the beginning of the new heavens and the new earth. Nothing like it has happened in history. It will go far beyond the exodus and the flood, which are two of the most visibly dramatic events in history. Considering what He has done in the past, God's work at the end of the age will probably be shocking.

If the first coming of Jesus contained startling surprises, then the second coming will also.

The Pharisees knew the Bible better than most Christians, but they would not cooperate with God's work in their generation because it was not what they expected. Most of us do not know the Bible as well as they did, but we are convinced we know precisely what God will do and how He will fulfill His promises. We tend to be arrogant toward the Pharisees, castigating them for their blindness but never considering how we will respond if the Lord surprises us in the way He fulfills the rest of His promises when He comes again.

Every time God has done something dramatic in history, a number of people have been severely offended. This is a sober warning to us because the return of Jesus is the most visibly dramatic and astonishing event yet, so much so the prophets found human language incapable of fully describing what is coming.[6]

If we knew everything God is doing, like Isaiah and Habakkuk, we might be tempted not to believe the report.

I Have Answered Your Prayers

Habakkuk's complaint began with his frustration as an intercessor. He accused God of not responding to his intercession because he could not see God doing anything. God specifically addressed this complaint by commanding Habakkuk to "look!" and "see!" what He was doing. God spoke words that Habakkuk longed to hear, "I am doing a work in

---

[6]Job 20:28; 21:30; Psalm 110:3, 5; 118:24; Proverbs 16:4; Song of Solomon 3:11; Isaiah 2:11–12, 17, 20; 3:7, 18; 4:1–2; 5:30; 7:18, 21, 23; 10:20, 27; 11:10–11; 12:1, 4; 13:6, 9, 13; 17:4, 7, 9; 19:6, 18–19, 21, 23–24; 24:21; 25:9; 26:1; 27:1–2, 12–13; 28:5; 29:18; 30:23, 25–36; 31:7; 34:8; 52:6; 61:12; 63:4; Jeremiah 4:9; 25:33; 30:7–8; 46:10; 48:41; 49:22, 26; 50:30; Lamentations 1:12; 2:1, 22; Ezekiel 7:19; 13:5; 30:3, 9; 38:10, 14, 19; 39:11, 22; 45:22; 48:35; Hosea 1:5; 2:16, 18, 21; Joel 1:15; 2:1, 11, 31; 3:14, 18; Amos 2:16; 5:18, 20; 6:3; 8:3, 9, 13; 9:11; Obadiah 1:8, 15; Micah 2:4; 4:6; 5:10; 7:11–12; Nahum 1:7; Habakkuk 3:16; Zephaniah 1:7–8, 10, 14–15, 18; 2:2–3; 3:8, 11, 16; Zechariah 2:11; 3:10; 9:16; 12:3–4, 6, 8–9, 11; 13:1–2, 4; 14:1, 3–4, 6, 8–9, 13, 20–21; Malachi 3:2; 4:1, 3, 5.

your days" to answer Habakkuk's accusation. God had not ignored Habakkuk's prayers. He was not silent and uninvolved. God was actively at work.

God's answer was a rebuke to the charge that He had not answered Habakkuk's intercession.

If we do not recognize this crisis over intercession, we will miss the full message in the Lord's answer. God's response to Habakkuk could be reworded this way, "You accused Me of not answering your intercession. But I have answered your prayers. I am at work. I am directly involved. However, your assumptions have kept you from seeing what I am doing and kept you from recognizing the answer to your own prayers. I have responded to your intercession. In fact, your prayers have played a key role in My work among the nations. But I am not answering your prayers according to your personal expectations, hopes, and assumptions. I will accomplish My word, but I am not bound by your opinions of how I should lead. Look again at the nations and be confounded at the answer to your own prayers."

God's response revealed the assumptions in Habakkuk's prayers. When Habakkuk prayed for revival in his nation, he assumed God would answer with economic prosperity, political stability, and the defeat of Judah's enemies. Habakkuk was very confident about God's agenda for his nation. He knew the nation was in compromise, but he believed revival would address compromise and restore prosperity to the nation. *These assumptions kept Habakkuk from seeing the actual answer to his prayer.*

God's response to Habakkuk reveals the profound dignity of intercession. We can pray for the wrong outcomes with wrong assumptions and lack of understanding, and God will still respond.

Habakkuk had prayed with expectations that were misguided and completely out of step with God's purposes; he had asked God to prevent the very thing that would accomplish God's purposes. Despite this, Habakkuk's prayers had set God's purpose into motion. God did not ignore Habakkuk's prayers. He was not silent. He was actively responding to misinformed intercession. Ironically, Habakkuk's intercession had set into motion the very thing Habakkuk feared.

God *was* actively answering Habakkuk's prayers, doing the very thing Habakkuk accused Him of not doing. Though Habakkuk's expectations were wrong, God had answered his intercession. Habakkuk's complaint was a demonstration of his blindness.

Even Prophets Can Be Blind

God refused to accommodate Habakkuk's sensibilities. God shocked Habakkuk and then forced Habakkuk to accept the full implications of what He had said. God did not leave Habakkuk any room for a personal interpretation; He made sure Habakkuk fully grasped exactly what He had said.

Habakkuk did not need a minor adjustment in his perspective. He did not need a bit of prophetic insight to make sense of the situation. He was blind, and God had to shatter his thinking.

God's rebuke reveals it is possible to be a true prophet and be blind.

Even true prophets can be blinded by their own assumptions. This is a sobering warning because a blind prophet is a dangerous thing. They can easily interpret correct information incorrectly, but because of their gift, people rarely challenge their interpretation. Because of this, prophets must be deeply rooted in the Word of God and have their words judged according to the Word.[7] This is an ongoing challenge because the gift of prophecy still operates and is necessary for healthy churches.[8]

The gift to reveal a secret or predict an event is not enough to establish a biblically sound prophetic ministry.

Prophets are supposed to discern the will of God, but if prophets have wrong assumptions, their discernment becomes distorted, and their prophecies can become unhelpful at best and dangerous at worst. This can even happen to prophets who genuinely love God and are seeking to follow His ways. To avoid this, prophets *must* prioritize the knowledge of God, they *must* be deeply grounded in the Scriptures, they *must* be willing to submit to the Scriptures above their own ideas and interpretations, and they *must* live in community with the Body.

Tragically, in our day, these elements are often missing because many assume a prophetic gift is enough to create a "prophet." As a result, many prophetic people can speak true words but then interpret

---

[7] Isaiah 8:20; 1 Corinthians 14:29; 1 Thessalonians 5:19–21; 1 John 4:1–3.

[8] Acts 11:27; 13:1; 15:32; 21:9–10; Romans 12:6; 1 Corinthians 12:28; 14:1, 39; Ephesians 4:11; 1 Thessalonians 5:20; 1 Timothy 1:18; 4:14.

these words incorrectly, give people false hopes, and unwittingly lead people astray.

Having a piece of correct information does not mean the interpretation of that information is automatically correct.

Having an incorrect interpretation does not automatically mean someone is a "false prophet," but it exposes a need for discipleship. Sadly, people are so enamored with prophetic gifts that they rarely challenge prophetic people according to the Word. This sets the Church up for failure and creates the possibility for people to prophesy when they cannot really "see."

AN UNTHINKABLE ANSWER

God's answer confronted Habakkuk's assumptions and contradicted his convictions. The prophet was looking for affirmation of his expectations and an explanation for why his prayer had gone unanswered, but God's response produced a tremendous conflict. When Habakkuk heard God's answer, it overwhelmed him.

Questions raged in Habakkuk's soul: *Is it possible so many things I assumed were wrong? Is it possible God is not who I thought He was? God would never do this—not the God I know. Is it possible reality is not the way I think it is —that my entire way of thinking is a facade, an illusion, and a deception?*

Filled with turmoil, Habakkuk faced an incredible test. Would he allow God to reshape his thinking and expose his blindness? Was he willing to let go of deep-seated convictions that he assumed were God's? Would he cling to a God of his own making—or would he submit to revelation?

Habakkuk refused to believe what he had just heard, but he could not deny God's voice had spoken. He was confronted by a side of God he had not known. God was not a national deity—a god who existed to defend and preserve Judah. YHWH was sovereign over the nations. Even wicked nations could accomplish His purposes because His purposes were bigger than Judah and *all* things—even the things Habakkuk feared most—were serving God's purposes.

Habakkuk's confidence was obvious when he challenged God, but now he had encountered the God of Isaiah 29:

> *"Therefore, behold, I will again do wonderful things with this people, with wonder upon wonder; and the wisdom of their wise men shall perish, and the discernment of their discerning men shall be hidden." (v. 14)*

Clinging to Human Wisdom

Habakkuk could not handle the tension of God's answer—it was too shocking. His assumptions were so thoroughly embedded that, instead of bearing the tension of what God had said, he responded to the Lord with another complaint.[1] He was unwilling to conceive of the idea that God would *use* Babylon, so instead he challenged God to judge Babylon. God's rebuke had been strong, but Habakkuk's assumptions were stronger.

Habakkuk stated his assumptions again, issued another complaint, and waited for God to respond a second time:

Are you not from everlasting, O LORD my God, my Holy One? We shall not die. O LORD, you have ordained them as a judgment, and you, O Rock, have established them for reproof. (Habakkuk 1:12)

I will take my stand at my watchpost and station myself on the tower, and look out to see what he will say to me, and what I will answer concerning my complaint. (2:1)

The conversation is a perfect example of how our assumptions can keep us from hearing what God is saying. Habakkuk was confident God would save Judah and destroy Babylon. Instead of thoughtfully considering what God had said, Habakkuk quickly changed the subject to something more familiar and more comforting. He was so confident in his assumptions that he rejected what the Lord had plainly said rather than bear the tension of what the Lord had said. He took refuge in his thinking, *I know God will judge the wicked. Babylon is wicked. Therefore, God will judge Babylon. He could not possibly mean what He just said. I must have missed something. There must be a better explanation.*

Habakkuk's response to the Lord revealed his wrestle. His crisis was not his inability to discern political events; it was an incomplete knowledge of God.

Habakkuk tried to use comfortable biblical truths to escape the tension of what God had revealed about Himself.

Before we critique Habakkuk, we need to ask if we do the same thing. Do we really view the world through a biblical lens? Do we *truly* live with the tension of all that God has said about Himself? Or do we

---

[1] Habakkuk 1:12–2:1.

view the world through a lens shaped by our own assumptions and "informed" by Bible verses?

Based on the sheer number of "explanations" we seek to help us avoid the straightforward meaning of many biblical passages, it is obvious we are not any different from Habakkuk.

I Will Look to See What the Lord Says

Habakkuk rejected the Lord's answer, but his response to the Lord also showed a fear of the Lord that is rare in our time:

> *I will take my stand at my watchpost and station myself on the tower, and look out to see what he will say to me, and what I will answer concerning my complaint. (Habakkuk 2:1)*

Through social media, we *constantly* speak bold words and have incredible confidence in bold opinions on things we know very little about. We are perhaps the most vocal generation in history. We can quickly dismiss authority figures and experts based on our own opinions. Tragically, we rarely consider our words and think nothing of causing incredible division through our use of words. We *want* to speak and be heard.

Habakkuk did not agree with the Lord, but he stood and waited for the Lord to speak. Habakkuk's response to the Lord is a rebuke to our way of thinking.

Even in the Church, there is a compulsive need to speak. Whenever anything remotely unusual happens, people feel an enormous desire to speak for the Lord even when He has not spoken. We call this "prophetic," but in reality it is little more than "prophetic opinions" and "visions of our own minds."[2] This generation is far too quick to speak for the Lord and, as a result, often claims divine weight for thoughts that are predominantly human. The result is a cheap prophetic that lacks the power of *thus saith the Lord*. It is not prophetic; it is meaningless noise that can be dangerous and even delusional.

If the Lord has not spoken, we must not speak for Him.

We must not forget that Jeremiah and others battled with "prophets" who assumed their thoughts were the Lord's thoughts.[3] These "prophets" were enemies of the real prophetic. The biblical

---

[2]Jeremiah 23:16.

[3]Jeremiah 23:9–40; 27:14; 28:15–17; 29:21–23, 31.

prophets were not quick to speak. They waited until the Lord spoke before they spoke on His behalf. We need to learn to bear the silence of the Lord.[4]

Words are powerful, and if we want our words to have weight, we must stop using them so freely and so cheaply. As James said, the tongue is the most difficult thing to control.[5] How many of us take that seriously and commit to a lifetime of holding our tongue and being slow to speak? Because we have not taken this seriously, our words are often unnecessary, divisive, lacking wisdom, and they produce little fruit.

Habakkuk was frustrated with the Lord, but he still sat and waited on the Lord to speak. He entered a wrestle with the Lord when the Lord confronted his opinions. We need to learn this same skill. When crisis comes, our lives take unusual turns, or the global order begins to shift, we should not be so quick to assume we know what God is doing. We should wait and be quiet and let Him speak. Like Habakkuk, we may find He is doing something very different from what we imagined.

Make the Message Plain

Habakkuk waited for God to speak, and then the Lord spoke again:

> *And the LORD answered me: "Write the vision; make it plain on tablets, so he may run who reads it. For still the vision awaits its appointed time; it hastens to the end—it will not lie. If it seems slow, wait for it; it will surely come; it will not delay. Behold, his soul is puffed up; it is not upright within him, but the righteous shall live by his faith." (Habakkuk 2:2–4)*

God's answer came with instructions that showed something critical was at stake. Habakkuk's complaint was much more than a private conversation between God and Habakkuk. Habakkuk's blindness was not unique to Habakkuk, and God's rebuke was not only

---

[4]I am speaking here of the desire to give "prophetic opinions" and have the answer for what the Lord is thinking. Believers should turn to the Bible for insight into God's ways and how to respond in obedience. Sometimes, the Lord seems silent because He has already given us what we need in His Word.

[5]James 3:1–12.

for Habakkuk. God had staged the conversation to expose a critical issue with His people—an issue that continues to this day.

Habakkuk was told to write down this interaction and make it plain, which meant easy to read and easy to understand. God called it a "vision," further emphasizing that the message is about what we see. If you can grasp the message, you will see. If you do not grasp the message, you can have a legitimate prophetic gift, but you won't really see. It is possible to read Bible verses, pray, and still not recognize God's activity right in front of you.

God wanted this message recorded in a way that was easy to understand and carried everywhere so that His people would see.

God wants people to read this message, be transformed by it, and then run with it so others can hear it. These instructions reveal how critical this little book is. There are very few messages in the Bible that God asks the writer to record in a certain way so people can rapidly spread it.

The message that God wanted Habakkuk to see was much bigger than the crisis in Habakkuk's lifetime. It was a message that would "hasten to the end," meaning this message was not ultimately about Habakkuk's crisis. It is a message that God's people must grapple with all the way to the end of the age. It will take time for God's plan to be revealed, and people will be tempted to neglect this message, but we must *wait* until the end for the message to unfold fully.

The Just Must Live by Faith

Habakkuk argued with God because he wanted the assurance that God would destroy Babylon and save Judah. Habakkuk wanted God to answer his anxiety and fear with a reasonable explanation that Habakkuk could accept. God's answer was not the one Habakkuk expected:

> *Behold, his soul is puffed up; it is not upright within him, but the righteous shall live by his faith. (Habakkuk 2:4)*

The first part of the verse was a reference to the proud and the wicked. In context, it was a reference to the Babylonians. It was an assurance to Habakkuk that God was not overlooking Babylon's sin and pride. It was not right, and God would address it, but God did not give Habakkuk the details he desperately wanted. Instead, He gave

Habakkuk a command: *If you want to be righteous, you must live by faith.* The verse compares two ways of living. The first part of the verse is a warning against pride, and the second is an exhortation to faith (trust). Those who choose faith will live, which means those who do not are destined for destruction.

God's command carried a serious implication. If you do not live by faith, you are living like the proud—the ones who have confidence in their own strength or their own understanding. The ones who are destined for judgment. The message was subtle but shocking. "Habakkuk, if you continue to evaluate Me and do not embrace the path of faith, you are proud. Your soul is puffed up. You are like the Babylonians, and your end will be the same."

Habakkuk seemed to agree with God, but his confidence in his assumptions was a demonstration of pride. It was the way of Babylon.

If you want to be righteous, you can only live by faith. Faith is confidence in what you do not yet see:

Now faith is the assurance of things hoped for, the conviction of things not seen. (Hebrews 11:1)

The message is clear: God's leadership of history will not always make sense as it unfolds. If you have faith, however, you will survive. *You will live.* The basis for our faith is simple: We put our faith in the Person of God. God confronted Habakkuk's pride by refusing to give Habakkuk an explanation for the way He was leading history. Habakkuk would have to trust a Person.

God gave Habakkuk a simple command: "If you want to live, you must have more confidence in Me than what you see with your own eyes and understand with your own mind."

If you will put your confidence in Him, you can live. If you do not live by faith, you will end up with your soul "puffed up" because your confidence in your own wisdom is the basis of pride. If you live this way as a believer, you will end up in offense. Many of us automatically assume we fully agree with God's wisdom because we have either avoided this test or not yet faced it.

If God's ways always seem totally reasonable to you, you are not fully walking by faith.

If God's leadership always makes sense to you, it does not require faith. If this were the case, God's leadership would be an implementation of your own wisdom. Faith is only required when His leadership does not make sense to us. Faith requires you to trust God's character over your own ability to comprehend Him and His ways. That trust cannot be rooted in your evaluation of Him. If it is, your basis for trust is your own mind, and that is not faith.

God's word to Habakkuk was stunning in its simplicity but staggering in its requirement. The command to faith exposed a critical point: *Humans do not have the capacity to evaluate God's ways.* God had corrected Habakkuk's first complaint, but Habakkuk refused the message and complained again. God's second response was a warning to Habakkuk, "You cannot survive [live] if you continue to trust your evaluation over what I have revealed to you. You must have more confidence in who I am than in your understanding of My ways."

We Live by Faith Not Agreement

When we are perplexed, we assume we can agree with God if He gives us an explanation. Something deep in us cries out, *"Why?"* when we cannot understand. We will see in a future chapter why this cry is so deep in the human heart and why God responds to it the way He does.

God did not give Habakkuk an explanation because He did not want Habakkuk's agreement with Him—He wanted Habakkuk's faith! If our agreement with God is the basis of our relationship with Him, He has to submit to our wisdom, and His ways have to seem reasonable to us. However, He is not a creature who must submit to our ways. We are the creatures who must submit to His ways. Children have to trust their parents because they do not have the capacity to fully evaluate their parents' wisdom. It is always painful to see a parent who only does what a child wants. It hurts the child and demeans the parent. The same is true when a man tries to make God submit to human wisdom.

To live by faith, we must put our own reason in submission to God Himself.

God aggressively confronted Habakkuk so Habakkuk could see the pride in his thinking. God wanted Habakkuk to trust Him based on who He is, not based on what He would do for Habakkuk or Habakkuk's people. We can see God's goodness through His work in our lives, but we cannot base our faith on our evaluation of our circumstances because we do not have the capacity to evaluate God's work correctly. In reality, all of God's work is for our good, but in the moment we often cannot perceive the good that God is working. That good can frequently be seen in hindsight but not always in the moment. The reason for this is simple: We cannot comprehend all His ways.

There are aspects of God's wisdom that are unknowable to us because He is Creator and we are creatures.

We must learn to submit and to trust Him as a simple acknowledgment of who He is and who we are. We must come to a place where we trust Him regardless of what the external evidences seem to say. A good parent will require a child to submit to the parent's wisdom for the child's own good. God requires us to submit to His wisdom for our good and His glory. It is right and fitting because of who God is *and* it brings us incredible blessing.

As long as we resist this, we are evaluating God according to our own wisdom, acting in the same pride that filled the Babylonians.

This issue of faith is so foundational to the gospel that Paul quoted Habakkuk 2:4 twice and alluded to it around twenty times in Romans and Galatians.[6] This is at the center of our faith. It is a test many have walked through, and the end-time church will walk through this in a way we cannot currently anticipate.

God warned Habakkuk what was at stake in living by faith and then asked him a hard question, "Will you love Me if I use Babylon to destroy Judah? Will you trust Me if I destroy your dream?"

Let the Earth Be Silent
Can you trust God when He does not make sense to you?

In chapter 2, God assured Habakkuk He would judge the wicked but required Habakkuk to trust His judgment and His timing. God required Habakkuk to submit to His wisdom, including God's strange decision to use Babylon to destroy Judah. God required Habakkuk to trust Him, even when He used wicked men to bring about His purposes.

Just as God predicted, Habakkuk was astounded and bewildered[7] by this answer to his prayer, but Habakkuk finally saw. The message

---

[6]Douglas A. Campbell, *Pauline Dogmatics: The Triumph of God's Love* (Grand Rapids, MI: William B. Eerdmans Publishing Company, 2020), 299.

[7]Habakkuk 1:5.

was clear. He had a choice to make. He could continue with his complaint, the way of pride and, ironically, the way of Babylon, or he could allow the Lord to open his eyes. Habakkuk found the confidence to trust God, and the Lord opened his eyes.

The very thing Habakkuk had feared most was going to serve God's purposes and set the stage for something majestic:

> *"For the earth will be filled with the knowledge of the glory of the LORD as the waters cover the sea." (Habakkuk 2:14)*

That glory would come in a way Habakkuk could not fathom, but he was convinced it would come. With his blindness removed, Habakkuk gave a warning and an instruction. First was his warning:

> *What profit is an idol when its maker has shaped it. . . ? For its maker trusts in his own creation when he makes speechless idols! (v. 18)*

We think of idols as small religious figures, but Habakkuk exposed another form of idolatry. The idol maker is the one who "trusts in his own creation." When we trust in our wisdom, we are idol makers, and our wisdom is the idol. This form of idolatry is second nature for humans (especially those shaped by the Enlightenment),[8] but it remains idolatry. It is even idolatry when it feels biblical and we use verses to support it.

Habakkuk finished the chapter with an instruction:

> *The LORD is in his holy temple; let all the earth keep silence before him. (v. 20)*

This was Habakkuk's answer. The uncreated God sits on His throne. *Let all creation be silent before Him.* Habakkuk had complained. He had challenged God twice. Now that his eyes were opened, he had only one response: *Keep silent.*

The encounter between Habakkuk and God was about seeing, but up to this point Habakkuk had only described a conversation. Now, Habakkuk described what He saw: the Lord enthroned in His temple. This was the answer to Habakkuk's crisis: *The Lord was seated in His*

---

[8]The Enlightenment is so significant we will consider how it has shaped our thinking in another chapter.

temple. God's majesty and sovereignty became the source of Habakkuk's confidence.

Habakkuk was not given an explanation for why God was using Babylon to overthrow Judah.[9] Habakkuk's only explanation was *God Himself*. Habakkuk's confidence was to rest on the fact that God is on His throne in His temple. His temple is not just His place of worship, but His place of sovereignty over the earth.

Our confidence in God does not rest in our present condition; it rests in the fact that God sits enthroned over the earth. God has not abdicated His throne. He has not left us. He remains in His holy temple. The wise should *keep silent*. This is not just a one-time act. No matter what comes, no matter what happens, no matter what we see, we must *keep* silent before Him. Our accusations against Him and our evaluations of His leadership are a demonstration of our pride, and they must cease and give way to confident faith.

When we are confident in our complaints but not in our faith, we have not learned Habakkuk's message.

This does not mean the people of God do not cry out in intercession. It does not mean suffering can only be endured in silence. It does not mean we cannot ask genuine questions in the pain and perplexity of a situation. Even Jesus cried out in His suffering.[10] It is a command, however, that our accusations must stop.

As God's people, we should be silent before Him *now* before the great and terrible day when He will make His judgments and silent all accusations in the earth:

> *Be silent before the Lord God! For the day of the Lord is near; the Lord has prepared a sacrifice and consecrated his guests. (Zephaniah 1:7)*

> *Be silent, all flesh, before the Lord, for he has roused himself from his holy dwelling. (2:13)*

> *When the Lamb opened the seventh seal, there was silence in heaven for about half an hour. (Revelation 8:1)*

---

[9]Habakkuk did understand Judah's precarious position according to the terms of the law, but he could not believe God would use Babylon to discipline Judah.

[10]Psalm 22:1; Matthew 27:46; Mark 15:34.

Habakkuk's complaint began with the demand for an answer. He did not "see" an explanation, however; He saw a Person. That was his answer.

THE SONG OF FAITH

When Habakkuk was delivered from his own wisdom, his heart burst into song. It is a majestic song that describes God coming in glory and judgment.[1] Above all, it is a song of *confidence*. Habakkuk's song is the grand crescendo of his book, and it is so significant that it takes up about a third of the book. One scholar referred to it as "the great theophany."[2]

Habakkuk's wrestle with God liberated him from his fear and anxiety. He expressed his newfound freedom with profound words:

Though the fig tree should not blossom, nor fruit be on the vines, the produce of the olive fail and the fields yield no food, the flock be cut off from the fold and there be no herd in the stalls, yet I will rejoice in the LORD; I will take joy in the God of my salvation. GOD, the Lord, is my strength; he makes my feet like the deer's; he makes me tread on my high places. To the choirmaster: with stringed instruments. (Habakkuk 3:17–19)

Ironically, when Habakkuk submitted to God's absolute sovereignty over the coming trouble, it released worship, rejoicing, and singing.

Habakkuk sang because he had finally found the comfort he desperately needed, but it was not the comfort he was longing for when he had first made his complaint. Like Habakkuk, we try to find comfort in our circumstances, and we long for answers that assure us

---

[1]It can be called "the longest and most detailed theophany (appearing of God) in the whole Old Testament." See Joel Richardson, *Sinai to Zion: The Untold Story of the Triumphant Return of Jesus* (Leawood: Winepress, 2020), 214.

[2]George Adam Smith, *The Book of the Twelve Prophets*, 2 vols. (London: Hodder and Stoughton, 1898), 2:150.

our lives will not be disrupted. But God does not give us the comfort we long for. Instead, He gives us a different comfort.

God is our only unshakable comfort in this age.

Habakkuk initially rejected God's response to him because Habakkuk was looking for comfort in his circumstances. Habakkuk simply could not believe that God was involved in the thing he feared most and at work in the looming calamity. Habakkuk was looking for assurance his circumstances would not be disrupted, but he discovered God was driving the disruption.

Like Jacob, Habakkuk wrestled with God until the light came. Habakkuk suddenly found comfort in the *Person* of God rather than his circumstances. Habakkuk realized if God is the one ultimately directing everything in this age, then everything will ultimately serve His good purposes. Habakkuk's discovery was both incredibly shocking *and* incredibly comforting. God does not endorse evil, nor does He completely explain how evil serves His purposes (we will see why in a future chapter), but He is enthroned above *everything* and intricately involved in everything in ways we simply cannot fathom. And He will judge evil completely, once it has served His purposes.

God's sovereignty does not answer every question, nor does it eliminate the pain of evil in this age. Nevertheless, evil cannot destroy God's purposes. We cannot always find hope in our circumstances, but we can find hope in Him and His purposes. He is *good* in ways we cannot imagine.[3] He *loves* us with desire we cannot fathom.[4] He is *fully committed* to our future glory with all His strength. He has promised we will rule with Him and become like Him.[5] God did not ignore Habakkuk's cry against injustice. God is more committed to justice than we are, and He expects us to share His zeal for justice. He does not overlook injustice, but He will bring justice His way.

This is our hope and our comfort: We have an all-powerful God who loves us with the deepest parts of His being and is fully committed to our future glory. This

---

[3]Ephesians 3:20–21; 1 Corinthians 2:9.

[4]John 17:23, 26; Romans 5:8; 8:37–39; Galatians 2:20; Ephesians 2:4; Colossians 3:12; 5:2, 25–27; 1 Thessalonians 1:4; 1 John 4:10.

[5]Daniel 7:27; Matthew 19:28–29; Romans 8:17; 2 Timothy 2:12.

does not resolve all the pain of evil in this age, but it gives us a rock solid and unshakable hope which is the basis of biblical comfort.

This is not just a message for Habakkuk; this is a message for us. Day by day, we continue to live with the effects of evil in our age. Many Christians live in places of affluence with relative peace and safety, and I fear we have forgotten the New Testament does not promise us prosperity, peace, or safety. On the contrary, the New Testament repeatedly predicts suffering will be common in this age.[6]

Moreover, we can see the season in the earth slowly turning toward the days that will directly precede Jesus' return. The Bible warns us these days will culminate in a time of crisis unlike any other time in history,[7] and many believers will lose their lives in the coming trouble.[8] We may or may not live through these days, but if we do not live through them, we must prepare the generations to come for them. Like Habakkuk, we must have a rock solid source of hope that gives our hearts profound comfort as we endure a calamity coming the likes of which the world has never seen—a crisis that will go far beyond the events that troubled Habakkuk.

The reality that God is intricately involved in history and using *everything* for His purposes gives us the confidence to face incredible trouble. This is the path to freedom because it means we have not been abandoned. Everything serves His purposes, and even evil cannot thwart His purposes.

God will get what He wants, and our future is secure in Him. Any other hope is superficial and flimsy.

When Habakkuk broke through to the knowledge of God, his circumstances did not change, but he began singing with confidence. When we discover this biblical hope, we will erupt in singing just like Habakkuk. Paul labored tirelessly among the Gentiles to see this singing people emerge.[9] Habakkuk's song was a foreshadowing of the

---

[6]Matthew 10:16–25; 16:21, 24; Mark 8:31, 34; 13:9–13; Luke 9:22–23; 24:26, 46; John 16:2, 33; Acts 14:22; Romans 8:17–18; Philippians 1:29; 3:10–11; Hebrews 2:10; 5:8; 1 Peter 2:19–21; 4:13–14, 19; 5:9–10; Revelation 2:10.

[7]Jeremiah 30:7; Daniel 12:1; Joel 2:2; Matthew 24:21.

[8]Revelation 6:11; 7:9–17; 12:11; 13:15; 17:6.

[9]Romans 15:9–12.

end-time church that will break through to the knowledge of God and then release an explosive song of praise during the most difficult period of this age:[10]

> *The earth mourns and withers; the world languishes and withers; the highest people of the earth languish. . . . The earth lies defiled under its inhabitants. . . . Therefore a curse devours the earth, and its inhabitants suffer for their guilt; therefore the inhabitants of the earth are scorched, and few men are left. . . . Desolation is left in the city; the gates are battered into ruins. For thus it shall be in the midst of the earth among the nations, as when an olive tree is beaten, as at the gleaning when the grape harvest is done. They lift up their voices, they sing for joy; over the majesty of the LORD they shout from the west. Therefore in the east give glory to the LORD; in the coastlands of the sea, give glory to the name of the LORD, the God of Israel. From the ends of the earth we hear songs of praise, of glory to the Righteous One. But I say, "I waste away, I waste away. Woe is me! For the traitors have betrayed, with betrayal the traitors have betrayed." (Isaiah 24:4–6, 12–16)*

God is forming a singing people in the nations who will release a roar of praise during the most difficult hour of history, but we need the knowledge of God that Habakkuk discovered to become that people.

Not only did Habakkuk worship, he also lifted his voice in intercession:

> *O LORD, I have heard the report of you, and your work, O LORD, do I fear. In the midst of the years revive it; in the midst of the years make it known; in wrath remember mercy. (Habakkuk 3:2)*

After Habakkuk's wrestle with God, he returned to the place of intercession. This time his intercession was not a complaint but a plea for mercy. His encounter with God convinced him of the rightness of God's judgments *and* of God's desire for mercy. He acknowledged God was at work in the nations and asked for mercy for his people. He

---

[10]Psalm 96:1, 9, 13; 98:1–9; 102:15–22; 122:6; 149:6–9; Isaiah 19:20–22; 24:14–16; 25:9; 26:1, 8–9; 27:2–5, 13; 30:18–19, 29, 32; 35:2, 10; 42:10–15; 43:26; 51:11; 52:8; 62:6–7; Jeremiah 31:7; Joel 2:12–17, 32; Zephaniah 2:1–3; Zechariah 8:20–23; 10:1; 12:10; 13:9; Matthew 21:13; Luke 18:7–8; Romans 15:8–11; Revelation 5:8; 8:3–5; 16:7; 22:17.

prayed with confidence because he knew God was intimately involved. God loves intercession for mercy when we are in agreement with Him.

Like Habakkuk, we need to discover what it takes to break through to biblical comfort, see God as He really is, and become a people who sing.

THE CHALLENGE OF ANSWERED PRAYER

Many people wrestle with offense over unanswered prayer, but Habakkuk discovered answered prayer can be more offensive than unanswered prayer.

When we pray, we nearly always form expectations about how our prayers will be answered. We pray with specific outcomes in mind, assuming the Lord agrees with our outcomes. Our expectations are not always wrong, but God often hears our prayers and then answers them in shocking and unexpected ways.

Habakkuk challenged God with a bold complaint: *"You are not answering my prayer."*

God gave a shocking response: *"I am responding to your prayer but answering it in a way you never expected. Your intercession played a part in My activity, but I did not act according to your assumptions."*

The conflict between God and Habakkuk shows the dignity of prayer. God took Habakkuk's prayers seriously and responded to them, even though Habakkuk did not understand God's ways and was actually in opposition to what God was doing in his generation. God is not looking for "perfect" intercession. A good parent engages a child who speaks confidently about wrong perceptions, and God intentionally engages His people when they do not know Him. He patiently moves His people from ignorance to maturity, and He intentionally engages with us. He *welcomes* our approach even when we do not grasp His ways.

God values intercession so much that it sets His work into motion even when we do not understand what He is doing. God's response to Habakkuk's intercession was not what Habakkuk expected, but God did respond.

What prayers are you praying that you have assumed are unanswered when in reality they may have set God into motion in a radically different way than you expected?

One of the major lessons of Habakkuk 1 is that God answers prayer. Many times, we are tempted to become bitter over unanswered prayer when the actual issue is that He has not answered our prayers in the way we expected. God responds to His people when we pray, but He responds according to His wisdom and not ours. He does not operate on our timelines, and He does not always answer prayer the way we expect.

Habakkuk discovered as prayer increases, the opportunity for offense also increases.

The God of Habakkuk Still Lives

Prayer is often fueled by fear. Whether a crisis is real or imagined, crisis drives people to the place of prayer. Many prayers for revival are really prayers to preserve economic prosperity, political stability, or a certain way of life we assume is God's best. We often presume our personal dreams are God's desires and ask God to preserve something we have or give us something we want, thus confusing our desires with "revival."

Habakkuk rejected God's first response because his prayer for revival was really a prayer to preserve Judah's status quo. Judah was corrupt, harbored injustice, and had been unfaithful to YHWH, but Habakkuk was convinced Judah was better than other nations. Habakkuk assumed God wanted to save the nation, and he likely used Bible verses to support his expectations.

God is not always committed to the same things we are committed to. In the mystery of God's leadership, the thing Habakkuk feared most was going to accomplish God's purposes.

Habakkuk never imagined God was not interested in preserving Judah's compromised state, but God's purposes were going to require the end of the political entity Habakkuk knew and loved. The destruction of Judah would serve a long-term purpose in God's plan to accomplish what He wanted, because God's story was bigger than Judah's success. God was working out a purpose that would extend beyond Habakkuk's life.

God's answer to Habakkuk is a warning to us today.

There has been more prayer for revival in the last few decades than ever in history, but it is easy to look around and ask, "Where is the revival?" We have not seen what we have hoped for (particularly in

many affluent nations). Instead of packed churches, in many place
see apathy in church, open hostility against the gospel, and rising
persecution after decades of prayer. Many of our revival prayers also
contain nationalistic hopes, but the nations are increasingly unstable,
and the global order is shifting. After years of prayer without the
expected answers, many are quietly asking, "Where is God? Why won't
He answer?"

*Like Habakkuk, it is time to ask an uncomfortable question: What if some
of the things we fear most are actually the work of God for the long-term formation
of His people?*

While churches are not packed to overflowing in every nation,
stunning things are happening. The political map is being redrawn in
many regions of the earth. New superpowers are emerging, and old
superpowers are fading. A financial crisis nearly brought down the
economic powers that have shaped the last fifty years. There are more
refugees in the earth now than at any point in history, and their
eventual resettlement will permanently alter many nations. For the first
time in history, a global pandemic has shut down the entire earth within
a few short weeks.

Things that were thought to be impossible only a few years ago are
now happening at an increasing pace. Each year seems to bring bigger
transitions than the year before. These transitions do not look like
"revival," but they are happening as a global prayer movement emerges.
The established world order that ruled for nearly fifty years has begun
to shift as global prayer has increased.

*This cannot be a coincidence. What if things we fear are an answer to the cry
for global revival?*

Humanistic thinking (particularly the Enlightenment) has affected
our thinking so much that we often pray, "Lord, break in," as if history
is following its own course and God needs to "break in" to redirect it.
We have forgotten that the God of Habakkuk still rules history.
Habakkuk prayed for preservation of his nation's status quo, but his
prayers set something much larger into motion. He could not recognize
what God was doing because it was so different from what he had
expected. What if we are in the same situation? What if God is
answering our prayers in a way we have never imagined?

What if God has taken our prayers for revival and the preservation of our current comforts and answered by disrupting the world and setting the stage for the return of His Son?

What if all the things in the earth that challenge us and frighten us are in reality signs of God's unprecedented activity to shape the world and set the context for something much, much bigger than we have been praying for? What if the unprecedented amount of prayer for "revival" has set something far bigger into motion that will include a final harvest, a great tribulation, the end of the age, and the return of the Divine Human to the earth?

God's redemptive goal does not minimize the incredible suffering present in our world nor erase the terrible things done by wicked men. We will address the challenge of evil more deeply in another chapter, but first we must soberly consider if our expectations—the ones we verbalize and the ones we hold subconsciously—have blinded us to what God is doing. Could we be like Habakkuk, accusing God of inactivity and gripped by fear and anxiety when in fact God has responded to us? Habakkuk was desperate to avoid a conflict with Babylon, but he learned God will take us places we would never go in response to our own intercession.

There are times we cannot see what God is doing because we are hoping to preserve something He does not want to preserve. Is it possible you are passionately praying for God to save things He does not want to save?

The Righteousness of God

We typically think of righteousness as moral perfection, but biblical righteousness is more than that. Someone is righteous if they are faithful to do everything they have promised and everything they should do. When the Bible says God is righteous, it means God will do everything He has said He will do. His righteousness implies a moral perfection, but God's faithfulness is at the heart of His righteousness.

When God told Habakkuk that He was raising up Babylon, Habakkuk faced a challenging question: Could Habakkuk believe God would perform all His promises to Israel even if God brought Israel into her promises in a way that Habakkuk would have never expected?

Habakkuk was not told God was going to abandon His promises to Israel, but God's plan to bring Israel to maturity was radically different from what Israel or Habakkuk could have even conceived.

God would be faithful to His promises, but that faithfulness would look radically different from what Habakkuk had assumed. Could Habakkuk trust God in calamity? Could Habakkuk trust God in the trauma of a military invasion? Could Habakkuk trust God if he saw war and not prosperity in his lifetime? Could Habakkuk die as a captive of Babylon with confidence that God would still fulfill all His promises?

Habakkuk was confronted with the message God gave Isaiah:

For when your judgments are in the earth, the inhabitants of the world learn righteousness. (Isaiah 26:9)

There are aspects of God's righteousness that are only discovered in His judgments. In His judgments, we discover His faithfulness to Himself. He really will answer sin and evil, even among His own people. In His judgments, we discover the mystery of His leadership because His judgments advance His purposes and set the stage for His salvation. This does not mean every individual will experience God's salvation. Individuals can suffer irreparable loss in God's judgments. Yet, God is *righteous* in His judgments, and they play a key role in fulfilling His promises. This is not easily understood, but it has been repeatedly demonstrated by God's work in the nations and in our own lives.

We learn His faithfulness when His judgments produce good that we never anticipated.[1]

We are so bound to time that we quickly forget we are part of an eternal story that is much bigger than anything that happens in our lifetimes. Abraham is *still waiting* on his promises because his story is connected to ours.[2] We have to think about the eternal story to avoid offense. You may or may not see the fulfillment of God's promises in your life. You may live through war or peace, but your life is your moment in this age to follow God by faith and intercede for His promises to come to pass, confident that a faithful life reverberates beyond a person's lifetime and that your intercession lives forever.

---

[1] We experience this in a very small way when crises in our lives end up producing profound growth.

[2] Hebrews 11:8–13, 39–40.

"O You of Little Faith"

Many of our prayers reveal we have the same fear that Habakkuk had. Deep down, we fear that God is distant, removed, and not really involved in our situation. God's answer to these fears is simple: "I hear you, and I act in response to your intercession. I am sovereign over the nations. My leadership does not make sense to you, but I can be trusted."

There was a time when Jesus and His disciples were caught in a big storm on the Sea of Galilee. The disciples were terrified as waves splashed into the boat, but Jesus was sleeping. In a panic, the disciples woke Jesus up, unable to understand how He could sleep in a storm. His first words were filled with affection and revealed He viewed the situation differently:

> *And he said to them, "Why are you afraid, O you of little faith?" Then he rose and rebuked the winds and the sea, and there was a great calm. (Matthew 8:26)*

The disciples knew Jesus had power, but when they felt the water, heard the wind, and were rocked by the waves, they were more affected by what they saw than what they knew. Jesus gave one simple instruction: *"I am with you—take more confidence in who I am than what you can see with your eyes."*

We are very good at reading biblical history and agreeing with what God said because we did not live through those events. We glibly describe the Babylonian invasion of Israel as the judgment of God, but we do not consider how horrific that invasion was and what Judah suffered. Jeremiah wept over mothers who ate their children,[3] but we read the story with little emotion. We even read biblical prophecies about the unprecedented end-time trouble that will come under the beast, and we easily affirm God's sovereignty over those events.

We are experts at applying the Bible in the past and the future, but we usually struggle to apply the Bible accurately in our generation. Like Habakkuk, we have entrenched assumptions that render us unable to see or even consider what God will or will not do in our time. Truthfully, we are often more moved by our fears and our expectations than what the Bible says.

---

[3] Lamentations 4:10.

We do not overtly reject Habakkuk's message, but we often fail to fully apply it, not realizing the failure to apply his message is essentially a rejection of it.

We correctly see Habakkuk as a "blind" prophet but assume we see clearly even when we hold assumptions that are strikingly similar to Habakkuk's. Our own blindness keeps us from fully grasping Habakkuk's message and recognizing the force of it. We find comfort in Bible verses used out of context, quickly forgetting Habakkuk also used Bible verses to back up his assumptions.

We often grow in anxiety and offense over "unanswered prayers" and rarely ask, "Could this be God?" We automatically assume God cannot be at work in world events if they include the disruption of something we hold dear even though this is precisely the message Habakkuk was given. We assume other people are "more wicked" than our people and some nations are "evil" but others are "good." We find it "unthinkable" that God would accomplish His purposes through the actions of evil or ambitious men, quickly forgetting the Babylonian invasion was just as "unthinkable" to Habakkuk.

We are quick to analyze Habakkuk's mistake and Israel's sins, but I wonder if God would say to us:

Why do you see the speck that is in your brother's eye, but do not notice the log that is in your own eye? (Matthew 7:3)

Could the things you fear most be part of God's leadership over your life? This question does not apply only to geopolitical disruptions. It can apply to the big *and* small events that affect our lives. What if the challenges we endure are not only the work of the enemy but also actions of God that are serving His purposes and will produce good for us?

God never asked Habakkuk to overlook or excuse Babylon's sin, nor did he ask Habakkuk to support Babylon. God does not ask us to agree with or promote wickedness, but He does demand we acknowledge His absolute sovereignty over everything. This is not an insignificant thing to God.

The Majesty, Mystery, and Controversy of God's Sovereignty

God's absolute leadership over history is one of the most controversial things in the Bible, but God repeatedly confronts people in the Bible with bold and controversial statements about His sovereignty over history. It is very important to God that we acknowledge His complete control over His creation and face the implications of His claims. If we do not seriously consider God's claims, we will have an incomplete knowledge of God.

God's control of history can be described as His sovereignty. God's sovereignty means many things to many people, but for our purposes we will define God's sovereignty as His absolute, governmental control over His creation. God is sovereign because He has absolute authority over His creation. His control is so absolute that, even when creatures do not obey Him, their actions still advance His purposes.

The doctrine of God's sovereignty has provoked men to study, ponder, and debate, but first of all it should provoke us to worship.

He Has Absolute Control

If you do not submit to what God says about His management of His creation, you will become blind and unable to fully see His work in your generation. Furthermore, your heart will become susceptible to offense.

Many people acknowledge God's sovereignty as an abstract doctrine, but God wants us to face all the implications of His claims, fully agree with Him, and be willing to live in the tensions it creates. God is not quiet about His sovereignty. Throughout the Scripture, He is very bold and open about His leadership over creation—both good and evil.

After suffering false accusations, slavery, and prison, Joseph realized that God had a purpose in his suffering:

As for you, you meant evil against me, but God meant it for good. . . . (Genesis 50:20)

The Lord warned Israel He would cause them to be defeated by their enemies, be gripped by confusion, wander the earth, and become an object of ridicule by the nations:

"The LORD will cause you to be defeated before your enemies. You shall go out one way against them and flee seven ways before them. And you shall be a horror to all the kingdoms of the earth. . . . The LORD will strike you with madness and blindness and confusion of mind, and you shall grope at noonday, as the blind grope in darkness, and you shall not prosper in your ways. And you shall be only oppressed and robbed continually, and there shall be no one to help you. . . . And you shall become a horror, a proverb, and a byword among all the peoples where the LORD will lead you away." (Deuteronomy 28:25, 28–29, 37)

God then promised to heal and restore Israel after Israel endures "blows" (or punishments) from God's own hand:

Moreover, the light of the moon will be as the light of the sun, and the light of the sun will be sevenfold, as the light of seven days, in the day when the LORD binds up the brokenness of his people, and heals the wounds inflicted by his blow. (Isaiah 30:26)

God addressed human arrogance by asserting He is in absolute control of His creation and directs it according to His desires:

"I am the LORD, and there is no other, besides me there is no God; I equip you, though you do not know me, that people may know, from the rising of the sun and from the west, that there is none besides me; I am the LORD, and there is no other. I form light and create darkness; I make well-being and create calamity; I am the LORD, who does all these things. . . . Woe to him who strives with him who formed him, a pot among earthen pots! Does the clay say to him who forms it, 'What are you making?' or 'Your work has no handles'? Woe to him who says to a father, 'What are you begetting?' or to a woman, 'With what are you in labor?'" Thus says the LORD, the Holy One of Israel, and the one who

formed him: *"Ask me of things to come; will you command me concerning my children and the work of my hands? I made the earth and created man on it; it was my hands that stretched out the heavens, and I commanded all their host." (Isaiah 45:5–7, 9–12)*

Hosea called Israel to return to the Lord and allow Him to heal her from the suffering He inflicted on Israel:

Come, let us return to the LORD; for he has torn us, that he may heal us; he has struck us down, and he will bind us up. (Hosea 6:1)

Amos warned Israel that disaster and calamity does not come unless the Lord has directed it:

Does a bird fall in a snare on the earth, when there is no trap for it? Does a snare spring up from the ground, when it has taken nothing? Is a trumpet blown in a city, and the people are not afraid? Does disaster come to a city, unless the LORD has done it? (Amos 3:5–6)

"I gave you cleanness of teeth in all your cities, and lack of bread in all your places, yet you did not return to me," declares the LORD. "I also withheld the rain from you when there were yet three months to the harvest; I would send rain on one city, and send no rain on another city; one field would have rain, and the field on which it did not rain would wither; so two or three cities would wander to another city to drink water, and would not be satisfied; yet you did not return to me," declares the LORD. "I struck you with blight and mildew; your many gardens and your vineyards, your fig trees and your olive trees the locust devoured; yet you did not return to me," declares the LORD. "I sent among you a pestilence after the manner of Egypt; I killed your young men with the sword, and carried away your horses, and I made the stench of your camp go up into your nostrils; yet you did not return to me," declares the LORD. "I overthrew some of you, as when God overthrew Sodom and Gomorrah, and you were as a brand plucked out of the burning; yet you did not return to me," declares the LORD. "Therefore thus I will do to you, O Israel; because I will do this to you, prepare to meet your God, O Israel!" For behold, he who forms the mountains and creates the wind, and declares to man what is his thought, who makes the morning darkness, and treads on the heights of the earth—the LORD, the God of hosts, is his name! (4:6–13)

Jeremiah warned Judah that people are made of clay, like pots, and God can do whatever He wants with the pots He has made:

And the vessel he was making of clay was spoiled in the potter's hand, and he reworked it into another vessel, as it seemed good to the potter to do. Then the word of the LORD came to me: "O house of Israel, can I not do with you as this potter has done? declares the LORD. Behold, like the clay in the potter's hand, so are you in my hand, O house of Israel." (Jeremiah 18:4–6)

God challenged Job's accusations against Him, and then Job's friends acknowledged the Lord had brought Job's trouble upon him:

Then the LORD answered Job out of the whirlwind and said: "Who is this that darkens counsel by words without knowledge?" (Job 38:1–2)

"Shall a faultfinder contend with the Almighty? He who argues with God, let him answer it." (40:2)

Then came to him all his brothers and sisters and all who had known him before, and ate bread with him in his house. And they showed him sympathy and comforted him for all the evil that the LORD had brought upon him. And each of them gave him a piece of money and a ring of gold. (42:11)

God does not answer all our questions about sin, suffering, and mystery, but He boldly claims absolute sovereignty over it all.[1] This is both profoundly comforting *and* incredibly offensive because we live with the effects of evil every day. Most people think about God's sovereignty with preconceived notions. They subconsciously assume the Bible does not mean what it plainly says and create explanations to blunt the implications of what God has said.

God does not give us the freedom to alter His words. He wants us to face what He has revealed about Himself even if we find it offensive. Our offense exposes a greater issue God wants to address.

We must face what God says about His management of creation if we want to know God *as He is*. If you want to know Him, it must begin with what He has revealed. It is impossible to know Him if you begin

---

[1]John Piper's book *Spectacular Sins* is an excellent resource on this subject.

with your own understanding. Our deeply held convictions and human reason are inaccurate and unreliable for defining reality, morality, ethics, or God because they have been shaped by fallen cultures and our own sinful nature. Our minds must be transformed,[2] but this only happens when our thinking is shaped according to what God has revealed.

There Are Questions God Will Not Answer

There are two basic reasons God does not answer every question we have about His leadership and evil:

1. *We cannot understand His governance of the cosmos.* Ever since the fall in the garden, humans have believed we can evaluate what is good and what is evil, but we do not have the capacity to do this. Just as an infant does not have the capacity to evaluate the decisions a parent makes on their behalf, so also we do not have the capacity to evaluate God's leadership. He is uncreated, and we have to acknowledge our limitations. The assumption we can evaluate good and evil is deeply ingrained in us, but this longing is the fruit of rebellion.

2. *God refuses to submit to human evaluation.* God does not mind honest, passionate questions, and He is incredibly sensitive to our plight, but He cannot be subject to our accusations and our evaluation of Him.[3] He does not owe us any answers for what He does because He is God. He does not exist as our servant; we exist for Him. Human accusations against God are an unthinkable arrogance, and God is not required to answer them. Humanity has put God on trial since the fall, but this is madness and human tyranny, and God will not—He must not—submit to it. If God submitted to it, He would be acknowledging our right to rule Him.

God has absolute control over everything in His creation, and everything serves His purposes, but what about evil? What do we do about that?

There are no easy answers to the subject of evil, but before we move forward, we need a basic biblical construct.

---

[2] Romans 12:2; 2 Corinthians 4:4.

[3] Isaiah 42:3; 63:9; Zechariah 2:8; Matthew 25:40, 45; Acts 9:4–5.

The Mystery of God's Leadership

When we read what God clearly and confidently says about His sovereignty, it raises a hard question: *Does this mean God initiates evil?* God's interaction with evil is a mysterious conundrum we cannot fully grasp, but we can arrive at a biblical framework for the subject based on what God has said.

Many of our debates over God's sovereignty would seem very strange to the biblical authors because they lived in a different culture and had a different worldview. They were comfortable with tensions that are unthinkable for Western thinkers. They assumed reality was defined by an all-powerful God who had revealed Himself. We trust our human perception to define reality and believe we can discern God, ethics, and morality through clear thinking and consideration of all available evidence. The prophets would be astounded by our humanism and consider our way of thinking incredibly arrogant. The biblical authors were perplexed by many of the same questions that trouble us, but their framework was entirely different.

Modern theologians often focus the conversation about God's sovereignty on the question of "determination," meaning who determines or causes things to happen. This question seems to create immediate contradictions. If God determines (initiates) everything, then it seems He is the author of evil, even though He is not.[4] If God does not determine (initiate) everything, then it seems other "wills" are influencing the direction of history. This, then, suggests God may not be sovereign. Some theologians solve this by proposing that every impulse must come from God or He is not sovereign over what He has made. Others solve this by presenting God as all-powerful and able to bring about an ultimate purpose but unable to lead history precisely. Much ink has been spilled on this debate as theologians try to explain the mystery of who God is.

In some cases, theologians are wrestling with questions the Bible does not answer because the Bible was not written by people who think the way we do. This is also why many of the answers the Bible gives to our deepest questions do not always make sense to us. *Instead of continuing to search for reasonable explanations and trying to resolve apparent conflicts, we need to allow the Bible to reshape our paradigm of reality.*

---

[4]James 1:13; 1 John 1:5.

We want to do our best to think about God's sovereignty the way the biblical authors did, so we will begin by defining God's sovereignty this way: *God has absolute, governmental control over everything He has created, including time itself. All creation serves His purposes. This means everything in creation will serve His predetermined outcomes, but it does not mean God is the source of every impulse in creation.*

Here are a few components necessary for a biblical view of God's sovereignty:

- God actively directs His creation toward His predetermined outcomes. God is not absent, and history is not open-ended.

- What God has decreed will be done. Every created thing will fulfill the purpose for which He made it.

- Every creature serves God's purposes, even if they are trying to resist Him.

- Within creation, God has given creatures the ability to make choices to love Him or resist Him. These responses to Him are genuine choices, meaning God is not the impulse of *every* choice a creature makes (though He is the motivating impulse in some choices).

- God holds creatures accountable for their choices, further showing these choices are real choices and not robotic actions.

The Sovereign God of Israel

God formed Israel to reveal Himself, so the story of Israel and the nations reveals how God's sovereignty works in history.

God formed Israel for Himself and chose to reveal Himself to the nations through Israel. God gave Israel a priestly assignment so Israel could fulfill this task: Israel was instructed to steward the presence of God so the knowledge of God would be revealed to the nations. Tragically, Israel failed at this assignment. (It is important that we say that Israel failed because of Israel's humanity, not because Israel was more evil than other peoples. Any people would have failed similarly.)

Israel repeatedly embraced the gods of the Gentiles or treated the Gentiles with disdain instead of inviting them to worship the God of Israel. Both sins seemed to prevent the knowledge of God spreading to the nations. The climax of Israel's sin came in the first century when

Israel's leaders partnered with Rome to execute Jesus. In that moment, it seemed like God's purpose for Israel had utterly failed. Then something shocking happened: After Israel's greatest sin, the knowledge of God suddenly and rapidly began expanding to the Gentiles.

Paul described how Israel fulfilled her calling through this unsettling turn of events:

> *Rather, through their trespass salvation has come to the Gentiles, so as to make Israel jealous. (Romans 11:11)*

Israel fulfilled her assignment through her rebellion (trespass). When Israel resisted God and committed the most serious sin in her history, Israel still fulfilled her God-given assignment, and this is a biblical example of the mystery and majesty of God's sovereignty.

God had decreed a purpose for Israel: Through Israel, the knowledge of God was to go to the nations. If Israel had been fully obedient to God, she would have been a light among the nations, and the nations would have discovered the knowledge of God. However, Israel was not obedient. Israel rebelled against God, including becoming a party to the worst sin imaginable. And then, because of Israel's rebellion, the knowledge of God rapidly spread out into the nations, and *in her sin* Israel accomplished her assignment.

God had decreed that He would be revealed to the Gentiles through Israel, and He gave Israel instructions to fulfill this assignment. Israel, however, disobeyed God and still accomplished her divine purpose. God did not initiate Israel's disobedience, nor was He the impulse behind her rebellion, but He remained sovereign over the assignment He had given Israel. If Israel had obeyed God, she would have fulfilled her assignment, and when she disobeyed God, she still fulfilled her assignment. This is how mysterious and profound the sovereignty of God is.

Israel's story reveals the core meaning of God's sovereignty: Everything God has created will accomplish what He wants whether they resist Him or cooperate with Him.

God does not explain how His absolute will for creation works with our ability to freely resist Him. The Bible plainly presents God's absolute control and also instructs us to respond to Him and choose His ways. There is a mystery we cannot comprehend where people and spiritual powers can decide to resist God or cooperate with Him, and their rebellion and obedience *both* accomplish His purposes. God determined to reveal Himself to the nations through Israel whether Israel cooperated with Him or resisted Him.

We can see a similar picture of God's sovereignty at work among the Gentiles. God has given the Gentiles an assignment to provoke Israel to return to Him.[5] God expects gentile believers to understand this assignment, show intentional kindness to Israel, and provoke Israel to return to Him. The Bible, however, contains a sober warning of a coming day when Gentiles will rebel against God and seek the end of Israel. They will form a military coalition that will lay siege to Jerusalem and oppress the Jewish people in an unprecedented way.[6] This will be a bold defiance of God's plan for Israel, but intensity of this time of trouble will fulfill His purposes by provoking Israel to turn to God and cry out for salvation.

The Gentiles have an assignment to provoke Israel, and it will be accomplished in the Gentiles' obedience *and* in their disobedience. The Gentiles who obey God will express His love to Israel and play a part in His pursuit of Israel. The Gentiles who rebel against God will get caught up in a rage against Israel, and that rage will provoke Israel to return to her God.

The summary of these assignments for Israel and the nations is profound:

- The Israelites who obeyed God played a part in God's revelation of Himself to the Gentiles through Israel.

- The Israelites who rebelled against God have played a part in God's revelation of Himself to the nations through Israel.

- The Gentiles who obey God will provoke Israel to return to God.

- The Gentiles who rebel against God will provoke Israel to return to God.

---

[5]Deuteronomy 32:21; Romans 10:19–21; 11:11, 13–14.

[6]Psalm 98; Isaiah 13:8; 34; Jeremiah 30:5–7; Daniel 7:21–22; 12:1; Joel 3:1–16; Zechariah 12:2–3; 13:8–9; 14:1–4, 9, 11; Matthew 24:15–30; Revelation 11:2; 12:13.

God's assignments to Israel and the Gentiles demonstrate the profound mystery of His sovereignty. Humans can make real choices to obey Him or resist Him, but no matter what they choose, they will accomplish the purposes He has decreed for them.

The Tension of His Sovereignty

God's sovereignty does not mean we overlook or minimize evil. God did not ask Habakkuk to overlook Babylon's evil, nor did he ask Habakkuk to celebrate Babylon's invasion of Judah. On the other hand, God required Habakkuk to submit to His leadership over all history. We must be grieved over evil, resist evil, and speak against evil while also submitting to God's profound sovereignty over history.

The prophets boldly proclaimed God's sovereign leadership, but they also wept.

Submitting to God's leadership will not answer every question or soothe all our pain. We will not find an immediate redemptive purpose in every evil act, nor should we attempt to. When someone experiences pure evil, we should not try to soothe their pain with a premature admonition that "all things work together for good."

We can find hope in God's total dominion over His creation, but we must not overlook the trauma and great suffering caused by the sin of men and the rebellion of evil spiritual beings.[7] Our knowledge of God's sovereignty does not and should not eliminate the raw grief and pain we feel as we encounter evil.

Will You Worship?

Evil men and evil powers are tools in God's hand, and God demonstrates His majesty and His supremacy by accomplishing His purposes through His enemies without violating their wills.

His enemies do everything they can to resist Him, and yet they ultimately serve His purposes. The way God advances His purpose through creatures who do evil is revolting to many, but it is the result of God's decision to give humans real dominion over the earth and empower them to make real choices. Humanity and spiritual beings will serve God's predetermined purposes, but He also allows them to resist Him.

When we read the Bible, our minds should explode, and our hearts should exclaim as we ask, "Who is like Him?"

---

[7]Romans 8:38; Ephesians 1:21; 3:10; Colossians 1:16.

God determined His purposes and then created creatures to accomplish those purposes. He gave those creatures the ability to make choices so they could partner with Him in a real relationship and experience genuine love. Many of His creatures love Him deeply, obey Him wholeheartedly, and serve His purposes. Simultaneously, billions of people and several spiritual powers make choices every day to resist God, and in their rebellion, they still accomplish His will!

Who can do this? Who can lead history this way? Who can create creatures and give them real choices and a real ability to resist and yet accomplish His purposes without violating their freedom or choice or His own character?

It is totally unthinkable. It goes beyond anything the human mind can comprehend. *And this is precisely the point.* Biblical sovereignty does not lead to debates—it leads to worship. Once we comprehend His leadership of His creation, we should fall down in absolute worship. His ways are incomprehensible to the human mind, and yet it is demonstrably true that His enemies accomplish His will.

If you have not fallen on your knees in worship at the majesty of God's sovereignty, you have not fully grasped it.

The question of God's sovereignty goes directly to the heart of the rift between God and man. This conflict is the focus of one of the oldest and most unnerving stories in the Bible, and that is where we will go next.

God's Answer to the Human Crisis

God's conversation with Habakkuk is not the first time God has confronted one of His friends. One of the oldest books in the Bible contains an even more shocking confrontation. The book of Job is one of the more perplexing books in the Bible. It is more than an old story. It is a *foundational* book written down thousands of years ago to give us insight into the knowledge of God. The book of Job is typically placed near the middle of the Old Testament, and we can easily overlook how significant it is.

The book of Job is set in the time of the patriarchs, before Abraham and the story of Israel.[1] As an ancient story from the beginning of human history, Job summarizes the human predicament and identifies our fundamental crisis. Little is known about Job, and that ambiguity serves an important purpose. Because Job is not a part of any other biblical story, and not identified with any specific people, it becomes a universal story that applies to everyone, everywhere—in all times. The book also does not have a known author to emphasize the fact that *God is the author of the message*:

> The identity of the author is totally eclipsed by the majesty and message of the book, adding to the mystery of the book: it cannot be associated with a single individual in history. All we know is that God gave it to us.[2]

Many people look to Job for answers about suffering, but surprisingly the book does not contain the answers most people are

---

[1] Michael L. Brown, *Job: The Faith to Challenge God: A New Translation and Commentary* (Peabody, MA: Hendrickson Academic, 2019), 11.

[2] Michael L. Brown, *Job: The Faith to Challenge God*, 10.

looking for because the book is not primarily about suffering. The story of Job's suffering is a teaching tool used to address the foundational human dilemma in this age and God's response to our dilemma.

The main subject of the book is not Job; it is God:

> The primary subject under discussion throughout the book of Job is God. The concept of suffering is only a secondary subject, the catalyst for the discussion. The theme of Job is the nature and basis of the relationship between God and man— founded on faith in God's self-revelation as ultimate reality and God's Person as supremely worthy. The function of the book is to display the dynamics of the relationship between God and man.[3]

While the book contains a real story,[4] like many biblical stories, the story is being used to teach a message. There are many ways to read Job. Job can be seen as a symbol of the individual struggle or as a picture of Israel's experience of God's leadership.[5] These applications of Job have value, but the main subject of the book is God, and the book is designed to challenge what we think we know about God. As one scholar wrote:

> Nowhere else in the Bible is such an unrestrained demolition of the traditional image of God carried out as in Job's speeches, words that once let loose have continued to resonate for millennia. . . . In this book, however, God is not the only speech forcer. Job also forces God to speak, and that speech, as unpredictable as Job's own, dismantles Job's identity and world.[6]

---

[3]Layton Talbert, *Beyond Suffering: Discovering the Message of Job* (Greenville, SC: Bob Jones University Press, 2007), 22.

[4]Because the book is obviously designed to teach a message, some have proposed it may not be a real story, but other biblical authors affirm Job was a real man.

[5]For example, Andy Naselli's excellent book *From Typology to Doxology* demonstrates the profound parallels between Romans 11 and the book of Job.

[6]Carol A. Newsom, *The Book of Job: A Contest of Moral Imaginations* (New York: Oxford University Press, 2003), 31.

Job has been given to us to help us navigate the Lord's leadership of our lives, but there is much more to the book of Job. The book is a gift to the Church and a training manual to prepare the Church for the end-time crisis. The closer we get to the end, the more critical the book of Job will become. In His wisdom, one of the first books God gave us will be one of the most critical at the end.

We should read the book of Job as a prophetic book.

Job's world was prosperous and at peace when disaster came suddenly. Job's calamity is a prototype of the end of the age which will come suddenly and unexpectedly in a time when the world seems to be normal, peaceful, and prosperous.[7] In his calamity, Job represents the end-time church trying to navigate this time of great tribulation. Job's situation reveals the heart issues the end-time crisis will expose so we can address these issues in our own hearts before the crisis comes.

The book of Job defines a key crisis the end-time church will face.

Suffering will not be the only crisis at the end of the age. There is a bigger crisis that will come in the human heart. This crisis, and not suffering, is the main subject of Job. As we have already seen in Habakkuk, we are headed toward a divine "iceberg," and the story of Job is focused on that iceberg. The book of Job reveals God's answer to the crisis, but we must study that answer carefully because it is not the answer most people are searching for.

God gives four profound messages in the book of Job that together serve as the main message of the book. Each of these messages is crucial, and you must know each message if you want the knowledge of God and a heart free of offense.

I Started It

This introduction contains God's first message: "I started it."

The first message is found in Job 1:1–2:10. There is no indication Job has the information found in these two chapters, but these chapters frame the story, and the rest of the book should be read with these two chapters in mind.

The opening of the story is perhaps the most controversial part of the book:

Now there was a day when the sons of God came to present themselves before the LORD, and Satan also came among them. The LORD said

---

[7]Matthew 24:36–39; 1 Thessalonians 5:3.

to Satan, "From where have you come?" Satan answered the LORD and said, "From going to and fro on the earth, and from walking up and down on it." And the LORD said to Satan, "Have you considered my servant Job, that there is none like him on the earth, a blameless and upright man, who fears God and turns away from evil?" Then Satan answered the LORD and said, "Does Job fear God for no reason? Have you not put a hedge around him and his house and all that he has, on every side? You have blessed the work of his hands, and his possessions have increased in the land. But stretch out your hand and touch all that he has, and he will curse you to your face." And the LORD said to Satan, "Behold, all that he has is in your hand. Only against him do not stretch out your hand." So Satan went out from the presence of the LORD. (Job 1:6–12)

Verse 8 is especially astonishing, "Have you considered my servant Job?" Consider this slowly. Satan[8] did not suddenly attack Job; *God invited Satan to persecute Job.* The events that follow the invitation are outrageous. Satan manipulates the weather, stirs up invaders to destroy Job's possessions, kills several of Job's servants, and even kills Job's children. Before chapter one ends, the story is already overwhelming, and it is just beginning.

After bringing these calamities, Satan appeared before God again:

Again there was a day when the sons of God came to present themselves before the LORD, and Satan also came among them to present himself before the LORD. And the LORD said to Satan, "From where have you come?" Satan answered the LORD and said, "From going to and fro on the earth, and from walking up and down on it." And the LORD said to Satan, "Have you considered my servant Job, that there is none like him on the earth, a blameless and upright man, who fears God and turns away from evil? He still holds fast his integrity, although you incited me against him to destroy him without reason." Then Satan answered the LORD and said, "Skin for skin! All that a man has he will give for his life. But stretch out your hand and touch his bone and his flesh, and he will curse you to your face." And the LORD said to Satan, "Behold, he is in your hand; only spare his life." (Job 2:1–6)

---

[8]Note that "Satan" in the book of Job is a title and not a personal name. It can also be translated into English as "The Accuser" or "The Adversary."

The second conversation is just as unbelievable as the first. While Job was still reeling from the trauma of his loss, *God invited Satan to consider Job again.* Nothing can reduce the outrageous nature of this introduction. While we have to be careful not to malign God's character, the obvious message is that God is much, much more involved than we think.[9]

From the beginning, Job's book is much, much more controversial than Habakkuk's. Habakkuk disagreed with God's plan to bring judgment on Judah through Babylon, but Judah was corrupt, wicked, and poised for judgment. This was not the case with Job, however. God gave Job this glowing assessment twice: *"There is none like him on the earth, a blameless and upright man, who fears God and turns away from evil."*[10] The trouble Job encountered was not a covenant judgment for his wickedness, and this makes the book even more incomprehensible.

The introduction is obviously designed to shatter what we think we know about God. God's two interactions with Satan are unthinkable because they place God at the center of Job's crisis when He initiates Job's suffering. Satan is obviously an accuser with an evil nature, and he is eager to bring harm to Job, but he is presented as God's servant in the story. The implications are clear. The world is not spinning out of control. Satan is evil but not leading history and not free to do as he wishes.

History is unfolding at God's initiation and for His purposes. Evil has introduced great suffering, but God still controls His creation. *This is both comforting and extremely perplexing.* The message of Job is not veiled or mysterious. It was carefully and intentionally written to unnerve us. What we find here is something the human mind cannot comprehend, and *this is exactly the point.* God is getting at something very deep in the human psyche.

The introduction to Job makes it apparent God does not want to satisfy us with an answer to suffering; He wants to challenge everything we think we know about suffering and evil in this age.

---

[9]The introduction is shocking, but it is also not a formula. We cannot diminish how uncomfortable the message in the introduction is, but neither should we turn it into a formula to imply God should be blamed for everything tragic that happens.

[10]Job 1:8; 2:3.

This astonishing message is not just about Job; it is about us. The Bible predicts God will set up the end-time crisis, not Satan.[11] In fact, Satan does not want the great tribulation to come because it will end with his judgment.[12] The dragon will release his rage during the great tribulation, but the great tribulation is not the result of his rage; it results from God's leadership. This has serious implications for how we understand God's leadership in the future *and* His leadership now.

Are we willing to accept God's leadership when He takes us places we would not go or assume He would never take us? Are we willing to accept the way He leads our lives? This applies to all the small, everyday details of our lives we find difficult or offensive. The moments where we ask, "Where is God, and why is this happening?" Can we accept His leadership there? If we cannot accept God's leadership in the seemingly small things of our lives now, we will not make it when we find ourselves in the end-time crisis that God is going to bring.

Is it possible there are circumstances in your life that you would never choose or desperately want to avoid that are in fact designed by God to produce something in you that cannot come any other way? Could some of your biggest frustrations be part of God's plan for you?[13]

This does not mean we should be a passive people, nor should we abandon intercession, but we need a radical paradigm change regarding God's leadership of history.

All Your Human Wisdom Is Foolish

God's second message in the book of Job is simple: *All your human wisdom is foolish and out of touch with true reality.*

Job's calamity set into motion the longest part of the book of Job. The heart of this section lasts from chapter four to thirty-seven, and it contains a series of lengthy speeches by Job and his friends as they

---

[11]Isaiah 9:19; 45:7; 48:5; Daniel 7:25; Amos 3:6; Revelation 12:9.

[12]Revelation 19:20; 20:1–3, 10.

[13]It is impossible to deal with all the pastoral implications of Job in this book, but this does not mean that we adopt an attitude of passivity toward evil. For example, those in truly abusive situations should seek help and freedom. Job does not call us to passivity toward evil or toward those around us who are suffering. It simply confronts us with God's leadership in many areas of our lives where we assume He is absent.

attempt to explain Job's calamity. The logic in these speeches sounds very reasonable and mirrors answers many of us have heard or given to people perplexed by their situation. These speeches seem insightful, but God's conversation with Satan in the introduction reveals the wisdom of these speeches is nonsense.

Job and his friends may offer "good" answers, but they have no insight into what is really going on. These speeches contain seemingly reasonable but contradictory messages and show the bankrupt nature of human wisdom. From chapter to chapter, we find contradictions and arguments that all seem perceptive but ultimately offer no real hope. Even Job struggles to make sense of what is happening and cannot find an answer.

Chapter after chapter, we are forced to acknowledge how much of our "wisdom" is out of touch with what God is doing.

Many people read Job's book and think subconsciously, *Job's friends offered good explanations, but they did not apply in Job's case.* This completely misses the point. These speeches were not recorded to give us examples of wisdom that did not apply to Job because he was in an exceptional situation. These speeches were recorded to expose our lack of insight into God and His ways. When God rebuked Job's friends, He did not correct their arguments. He told them, *"My anger burns against you, for you have not spoken of me what is right."*[14] God's answer reveals their issue was not a lack of information. Their issue was they did not have a true knowledge of God.

I have never met anyone who enjoys this part of the book. Most people who read the book of Job find these speeches difficult, long, hard to read, and generally boring, and this experience is part of the message. *When we read this section, God wants us to experience what all our human wisdom sounds like to Him.* We are bored by these speeches because God is bored with all our insights and opinions. These speeches are long, boring, and out of touch with reality because they epitomize human wisdom.

God wants us to face the emptiness of our own wisdom, so He spent most of the book of Job exposing the insufficiency of it. This section is nearly eighty percent of the book, indicating how important this message is. God's first two messages to Job, "I started it" and

---

[14]Job 42:7.

"Your wisdom is foolish," set the stage for this third message. The third message is delivered by God directly to Job. It contains God's answer for Job's suffering, but it is not the answer Job was looking for.

I WILL NOT GIVE YOU THE ANSWER YOU WANT

After all the boring speeches, we find God's third message in Job: "I will not give you an answer for how I lead. I am your only answer."

People read Job looking for explanations, but Job was never given an explanation for his calamity. He was given an answer we can find in his conversation with God:

> *Then the LORD answered Job out of the whirlwind and said: "Who is this that darkens counsel by words without knowledge? Dress for action like a man; I will question you, and you make it known to me. Where were you when I laid the foundation of the earth? Tell me, if you have understanding. Who determined its measurements—surely you know! Or who stretched the line upon it? On what were its bases sunk, or who laid its cornerstone, when the morning stars sang together and all the sons of God shouted for joy?" (Job 38:1–7)*

> *"Do you give the horse his might? Do you clothe his neck with a mane? . . . Is it by your understanding that the hawk soars and spreads his wings toward the south? Is it at your command that the eagle mounts up and makes his nest on high?" (39:19, 26–27)*

The first few verses contain the heart of the message. "Job, who do you think you are? You have obscured true wisdom[1] and spoken words without knowledge. Do you really have the capacity to question Me? If so, I have some questions. Let's see if you can tell Me the

---

[1]The idea of "dark counsel" is that Job's ignorant words have obscured true wisdom instead of illuminating it. See Michael L. Brown, *Job: The Faith to Challenge God: A New Translation and Commentary* (Peabody, MA: Hendrickson Academic, 2019), 254.

answer." God followed with a torrent of questions that Job could not possibly answer to make it completely clear Job, as a creature, was totally out of his league.

God did not give Job an explanation but a challenge: "If you can create and govern a cosmos, then we can talk about My leadership. If you cannot, then you must acknowledge your role as a creature."

God never gave Job an answer. *God Himself was the answer.* This propensity to challenge and evaluate God is deeply rooted in us. This issue was not visible in Job's life as along as he prospered. It was exposed when he was reduced to weakness. There are times God must reduce us and break our confidence in our strength to challenge our "wisdom."

The conversation revealed the crux of the issue was not suffering. Job's suffering created pressure which exposed the issue God really wanted to address. God did not put Job under pressure because of a sinful act. God considered Job to be a *"blameless and upright man, fearing God and turning away from evil."*[2] God wanted us to see that even a blameless man can still wrestle with the fundamental human issue.

When Job could not fathom what God was doing, he wanted to honor God, but his questions produced an accusation: "If God is good, then why am I suffering?" Job's friends kept looking for some rational reason for Job's situation. They assumed there was a sin God wanted to punish, but God was not after Job's sin; He was after something much deeper—something in us all. When God exposes Job's issue, we should immediately realize that Job's real problem is also our problem.

We are supposed to read Job's story and see our own wrestle with God's leadership of our lives.

When Job encountered God, he immediately understood he was out of his league:

> *Then Job answered the LORD and said: "Behold, I am of small account; what shall I answer you? I lay my hand on my mouth. I have spoken once, and I will not answer; twice, but I will proceed no further." (Job 40:3–5)*

However, God's challenge continued:

---

[2]Job 1:8; 2:3.

And the LORD said to Job: "Shall a faultfinder contend with the Almighty? He who argues with God, let him answer it." . . . Then the Lord answered Job out of the whirlwind and said: "Dress for action like a man; I will question you, and you make it known to me. Will you even put me in the wrong? Will you condemn me that you may be in the right? Have you an arm like God, and can you thunder with a voice like his? Adorn yourself with majesty and dignity; clothe yourself with glory and splendor. Pour out the overflowings of your anger, and look on everyone who is proud and abase him. Look on everyone who is proud and bring him low and tread down the wicked where they stand. Hide them all in the dust together; bind their faces in the world below. Then will I also acknowledge to you that your own right hand can save you." (Job 40:1–2, 6–14)

"Who has first given to me, that I should repay him? Whatever is under the whole heaven is mine." (41:11)

God challenged Job to accept his limitation as a human. "Who are you to question Me? What grounds do you have for your challenge? Do you think you are My equal in wisdom, power, or might? Does creation obey you?" God did not address the details of Job's complaint. He addressed whether Job had the right to challenge God at all. God forced Job to face his humanity.

God's point is simple—man must accept his limitations as a creature.

Not only does God not owe us any explanations, if He gave us an explanation of His leadership, we could not understand it. We simply do not have the capacity. As creatures, we cannot even comprehend His ways:

Oh, the depth of the riches and wisdom and knowledge of God! How unsearchable are his judgments and how inscrutable his ways! (Romans 11:33)

God challenged Job and his friends to submit to what they themselves had said:[3]

---

[3]See also Job 9:10; 26:14; 33:13; 37:19, 23.

"As for me, I would seek God, and to God would I commit my cause, who does great things and unsearchable, marvelous things without number." (Job 5:8–9)

"Can you find out the deep things of God? Can you find out the limit of the Almighty? It is higher than heaven—what can you do? Deeper than Sheol—what can you know? Its measure is longer than the earth and broader than the sea." (11:7–9)

Job had to learn the message Nebuchadnezzar learned:

All the inhabitants of the earth are accounted as nothing, and he does according to his will among the host of heaven and among the inhabitants of the earth; and none can stay his hand or say to him, "What have you done?" (Daniel 4:35)

God was not holding back information from Job, forcing Job to trust Him. Job did not have the capacity to grasp God's leadership—and neither do we. Job did not need God to justify his situation. He needed to trust a God he could not understand.

I Am Your Answer

God forced Job to trust Him on the basis of His character, not Job's evaluation of His explanations.

God was the answer to Job's complaint, and when Job encountered God, it ended his complaint:

Then Job answered the LORD and said: "I know that you can do all things, and that no purpose of yours can be thwarted. 'Who is this that hides counsel without knowledge?' Therefore I have uttered what I did not understand, things too wonderful for me, which I did not know. 'Hear, and I will speak; I will question you, and you make it known to me.' I had heard of you by the hearing of the ear, but now my eye sees you; therefore I despise myself, and repent in dust and ashes." (Job 42:1–6)

Job's response is profound. He acknowledged the majesty of God's Divine Person. He spoke God's words back to Him followed by words of repentance, *"I have uttered what I did not understand, things too wonderful for me, which I did not know."* Job's repentance was simple, "When I challenged You, I did not realize my limitations, I had not considered Your majesty, and I did not realize how far beyond me You truly are."

Job's issue was his knowledge of God. Job did not repent for an act but for his evaluation of God.

Job's book is not principally about suffering. It is about our evaluation of God's governance of our lives when it does not make sense to us. Job's sin was his accusations against God, so the majesty, beauty, and all-consuming love of God was enough for Job. Job never received an explanation for his suffering, but his encounter with the Person of God gave him confidence in the God who presided over his life.

The sight of God answered Job's accusations without any explanations Job could understand. God would not let Job find comfort in his own understanding. Job could only find comfort in God's nature and character.

Job repented because this was the issue—the sin—that God had exposed. Job was an upright man, but there was something hidden in his heart that God wanted to challenge. It was exposed, and Job, to his credit, acknowledged it in humility and repentance. Like Habakkuk, Job's encounter with God produced repentance and worship.

God will not be evaluated. He will be worshipped and enjoyed.

God confronted Job because He loved him. God had to address this issue to bring Job to maturity. He was not being cruel with Job. We often try to avoid God's rebukes, but God rebukes the ones He loves.[4] He does not discipline his enemies this way. God's rebuke terrified Job, but God's silence is even more terrifying than His rebukes.

As soon as Job repented, God expressed His affection for Job and His anger at Job's friends:

> *After the LORD had spoken these words to Job, the LORD said to Eliphaz the Temanite: "My anger burns against you and against your two friends, for you have not spoken of me what is right, as my servant Job has. Now therefore take seven bulls and seven rams and go to my servant Job and offer up a burnt offering for yourselves. And my servant Job shall pray for you, for I will accept his prayer not to deal with you according to your folly. For you have not spoken of me what is right, as my servant Job has." (Job 42:7–8)*

---

[4] Proverbs 3:12; Hebrews 12:4–9.

God was angry at Job's friends because they had not spoken correctly about Him. Their words seemed to honor God, but their knowledge of God was deficient. They assumed human logic could answer Job's questions about God, but Job had to intercede for them to save them from God's judgment.

Do you have a knowledge of God capable of speaking rightly about what God did to Job? God expected Job's friends to understand Him this way, and He expects the same from us.

God will not live under our examination and our philosophical microscopes. He will assert His preeminence, not because He is proud, but because we must know Him on His terms, because He is the Creator. If any other human behaved like God, they would be arrogant, but God is not like us. He is infinitely good, and creation only flourishes when we submit to Him as Creator.

When we are confident in our own wisdom, we live in deception and blindness, assuming we grasp reality when in fact, like Job's friends, we are confident in an illusion of our making and do not grasp reality. Thousands of years of humans trying to rule the earth in their own wisdom has made this abundantly clear. And yet our rebellion persists.

I Will Bring Blessing

The book of Job ends with God's fourth message: "My plan is not designed to destroy you but bring you into blessing."

> *And the LORD restored the fortunes of Job, when he had prayed for his friends. And the LORD gave Job twice as much as he had before. . . . And the LORD blessed the latter days of Job more than his beginning. And he had 14,000 sheep, 6,000 camels, 1,000 yoke of oxen, and 1,000 female donkeys. He had also seven sons and three daughters. . . . And in all the land there were no women so beautiful as Job's daughters. And their father gave them an inheritance among their brothers. And after this Job lived 140 years, and saw his sons, and his sons' sons, four generations. And Job died, an old man, and full of days. (Job 42:10, 12–13, 15–17)*

God led Job into suffering, but His ultimate purpose for Job was a greater dimension of blessing. The book ends with this because God wants us to have confidence when we are in a trial that His intentions for us are ultimately *good* no matter what we experience in a moment.

This does not automatically erase the pain or the loss we may experience.

Job experienced real losses—painful losses—that were never explained in the book. God never gave Job an answer for the death of his children and his servants. Job's situation was not reversed, but his final situation was "twice" the blessing of his initial situation. God gave him more, though it was not what Job had before.

The book ends with the tension that God's blessing came as a result of God's leadership in Job's trial:

And they showed him sympathy and comforted him for all the evil that the LORD had brought upon him. (Job 42:11)

God did not apologize for Job's suffering, and the end of the book echoes the beginning—the Lord had brought calamity on Job. The book ends with an invitation to trust God's ultimate goodness in the midst of the unexplainable. Some things in this age will be explained in the age to come. Sometimes, we can see the Lord's work in crisis when we examine our lives in hindsight. Other times, we will never truly understand His ways. Yet, God is orchestrating all things for our ultimate good.

The Offensiveness of God

God led Job into calamity to produce a message through his life. Any message that costs a man immense suffering and the loss of his own children demands our attention. God will not lead everyone through the same suffering, but He expects us to respond to Job's book commensurate with what it cost Job to become a message for us.

God does not hide Himself, and He does not avoid our offense with Him. He loves us, but He will not cater to our opinions about Him. From the beginning to the end, the book of Job is a ruthless challenge to human concepts of "ethics" and "goodness." The book is raw and designed to address a fundamental human issue: our desire to evaluate God. This is an "iceberg" in the human heart that will sink us if we do not see it coming and address it now.

God demanded that Job submit his reason to God's leadership on the basis of God's identity as God.

God's demand that we submit to Him and trust His goodness even while suffering is incredibly offensive to the human mind. God wants to expose this offense and force us to resolve it. He wants to break our human conception of reality so we will rebuild our entire framework of reality on what He has said and not what we perceive.

We are shaped by views of reality largely shaped by human attempts to interpret our experience, but if you want to define reality properly, you have to start with God and allow God to be God.

God gave Job the same message He gave Isaiah.

> *A voice says, "Cry!" And I said, "What shall I cry?" All flesh is grass, and all its beauty is like the flower of the field. The grass withers, the flower fades when the breath of the LORD blows on it; surely the people are grass. . . . Who has measured the waters in the hollow of his hand and marked off the heavens with a span, enclosed the dust of the earth in a measure and weighed the mountains in scales and the hills in a balance? Who has measured the Spirit of the LORD, or what man shows him his counsel? Whom did he consult, and who made him understand? Who taught him the path of justice, and taught him knowledge, and showed him the way of understanding? Behold, the nations are like a drop from a bucket, and are accounted as the dust on the scales; behold, he takes up the coastlands like fine dust. . . . All the nations are as nothing before him, they are accounted by him as less than nothing and emptiness. To whom then will you liken God, or what likeness compare with him? . . . Do you not know? Do you not hear? Has it not been told you from the beginning? Have you not understood from the foundations of the earth? It is he who sits above the circle of the earth, and its inhabitants are like grasshoppers; who stretches out the heavens like a curtain, and spreads them like a tent to dwell in; who brings princes to nothing, and makes the rulers of the earth as emptiness. . . . To whom then will you compare me, that I should be like him? says the Holy One. Lift up your eyes on high and see: who created these? He who brings out their host by number, calling them all by name; by the greatness of his might and because he is strong in power, not one is missing. (Isaiah 40:6–7, 12–15, 17–18, 21–23, 25–26)*

John the Baptist used Isaiah's words to prepare Israel for Jesus' first coming, and these words must be used again to prepare the earth for Jesus' return.

Most people find Job's calamity almost unthinkable, but the end-time crisis will be much more devastating than Job's crisis.

And no one has faced the trial that is coming. No one has ever lived in a time when Satan gives *all* his power to a human being for a brief period of time. This crisis will be so severe that Jesus will stop it short so people can survive.[5] Many of us are very confident we would not accuse God like Job did, but we have never faced a trial like Job had.

Considering how easily offended we are when people mistreat us or fail to honor us, can we honestly say we are prepared for what's coming?

Most people do not realize how many accusations they have against God's leadership of their lives, but our controversy with God's leadership will be inescapable in the days ahead. The Bible predicts history is going somewhere we cannot fathom. No one will think God's leadership of the end-time crisis will be "reasonable." If you take the book of Revelation literally (and there is no reason not to), half of the world's population will not survive what is coming. Jesus warned us the crisis would come suddenly, and we must live prepared for it.[6]

If the end-time crisis does not come in our lifetimes, other crises will come. There are parts of the world that have enjoyed relative peace, unprecedented affluence, and lack of conflict for a generation or more. If you have lived in this kind of context, it is easy to assume this is normal, but it is historically abnormal. It will not last forever. The Bible does not promise peace or affluence in this age. Jesus warned us trouble would come, and the cycles of history give us the same warning.[7]

We must resolve our offense now. God must deal with this in His Church *before* the crisis comes because He will have an overcoming Church at the end of the age.[8]

Why won't He simply explain His ways to us? This question goes right to the heart of the human issue, and that is where we have to go next. Most people think the antichrist is the biggest challenge the world

---

[5]Matthew 24:22; Mark 13:20.

[6]Matthew 24:32–33; 38–44; 25:13.

[7]Matthew 10:17–22; 24:6–10; Mark 13:9–13; Luke 21:12, 16–18; John 15:20; 16:2.

[8]Revelation 7:9; 12:11.

will face before Jesus' return, but there is another challenge most believers are unprepared for: *God's leadership.*

How can we love a God who leads history this way?

The good news is God has given us an unshakable reason why He deserves our complete trust. We will look at that reason shortly, but first we need to consider the issue Job's story exposes—the "iceberg" God must confront.

EXPOSING THE ROOT ISSUE

Why was God so direct with Job? Why did He shock Habakkuk?

God confronted Habakkuk and Job because He loved them. God confronted them directly and forcefully because their issue is at the basis of all sin and darkness in this age, but it is rarely identified or addressed. Until this issue is addressed, we cannot transition to the age to come, and humankind cannot be fully restored to God.

To identify this issue and root it out of our lives, we have to go back to a beautiful garden.

A Beautiful Garden and a Terrible Lie

When the serpent turned against God, he decided to destroy God's prize creation, the creature God had made in His own image.[1] He needed a way to corrupt man and turn him against God, so he decided to plant an accusation against God in the human heart that was so deep that it completely fractured the relationship between God and man.

With a scheme formed, he approached Eve with a tantalizing accusation against God:

> *Now the serpent was more crafty than any other beast of the field that the LORD God had made. He said to the woman, "Did God actually say, 'You shall not eat of any tree in the garden'?" And the woman said to the serpent, "We may eat of the fruit of the trees in the garden, but God said, 'You shall not eat of the fruit of the tree that is in the midst of the garden, neither shall you touch it, lest you die.'" But the serpent said to the woman, "You will not surely die. For God knows that when you eat of it your eyes will be opened, and you will be like God, knowing good and evil." So when the woman saw that the tree was good for food, and that it was a delight to the eyes, and that the tree was to be desired to*

---

[1]Genesis 1:26; 5:1; 9:6.

make one wise, she took of its fruit and ate, and she also gave some to her husband who was with her, and he ate. (Genesis 3:1–6)

The serpent planted a question in Eve's mind, "Eve, God created a beautiful tree with good fruit and then told you not to take the good fruit. Look at this fruit. Why would God tell you not to eat what is good?"

Eve saw the fruit was "good for food," and it was a "delight to the eyes." The fruit offered nourishment and pleasure, so why would God create this tree and withhold it from Eve? As Eve gazed at the fruit, God's commandment to not eat the tree's fruit suddenly did not make sense. God had said not to eat from this tree, but *why?*

Eve knew from experience that fruit was made to be eaten, and this fruit looked good. Everything Eve could perceive led to one conclusion: "I should eat this. It will benefit me." However, God had said, *"Do not eat this."*

Eve suddenly faced a crisis: Would she trust *her* evaluation or *God's?* Would she trust everything she knew, everything she could perceive, and everything she had experienced? Or would she trust what God had said even though it did not make sense to her and was not confirmed by her perception of reality?

The serpent knew Eve was struggling with a conflict between her perception and God's command, so he added an accusation to his question. "Eve, God's command does not make sense because there are things He is withholding from you. Trust your instinct. Trust your perception. If you act on what you perceive, it will open up a new world to you. Your eyes will be open. Instead of being dependent on God to define good and evil, you will be able to evaluate what is good and what is evil." The serpent did not just offer Eve the ability to know what good and evil were; he offered Eve the God-like ability to *evaluate* her circumstances and determine what is good and what is evil.

The accusation went into Eve's heart like an arrow. "Everything I can perceive tells me the fruit is good. There is no good reason for God to forbid this fruit." Eve evaluated God's prohibition again. Would she choose her perception of reality or what God had said? The moment of decision came, and Eve took one more look at the fruit. She carefully considered what she saw and everything she knew about fruit and life in the garden. She compared it one more time with what God had said—an instruction that did not make sense.

Then she decided to trust her own perception over what God had said.

When people think about sin, they think about all the wrong deeds, but evil deeds are not the *essence* of sin. They are an *expression* of the root. The root of sin is simple: choosing what we perceive to be good over what God has said. If God has prohibited something, but we perceive it would be to our good, we sin when we choose what we feel. If God has commanded it, but we perceive it is to our benefit not to do it, we sin when we do not do what He has commanded.

All sin flows from decisions to evaluate God on the basis of our own wisdom, understanding, and perception and to choose our evaluation over what He has said.

Going Beyond the Limits of a Creature

The serpent tempted Eve to go beyond her ability as a creature, because humans do not have the capacity to evaluate what is ultimately good and evil. It is impossible for a created being to evaluate every possible option, know what decisions will produce over time, and then determine what is truly good and truly evil. Only God has that ability, but we are made so much like God that we are tempted to take on something only God can do.

The great tragedy of it all is that God *does* plan to exalt us to a place we cannot imagine, but that exaltation requires us to trust Him so He can transform us into His likeness. *God cannot exalt us unless we become like Him.* The Person of Jesus reveals what God is like in human form, so He is the ultimate image of what we are to become. Jesus' exaltation came through a process no one would have imagined and a process no one—not even Jesus' disciples—agreed with.[2] If we want to be exalted with Him, we must submit to the Father's leading of our lives, and we should not be surprised if it appears just as perplexing as His plan for Jesus' exaltation.

The temptation to evaluate God is ultimately a temptation to break free of our limitations as a creature and take on Godhood for ourselves.

We can take what God has revealed to make wise decisions and just judgments, but that is the ability to *discern* good and evil, which is different from the ability to *determine* good and evil. Humans do not

---

[2]Matthew 16:22; Mark 8:32.

have the capacity to determine good and evil, but we are constantly tempted to step beyond the boundary of our own humanity and dabble in the things that only belong to divinity.

The fact the serpent was able to corrupt the entire human race on this one issue tells us how significant it is. This issue caused man to fall in the garden, it causes man to reject God every day, and at the end of the age, it will cause millions to fall away from God, including some who currently attend churches.

You may not engage in "sinful" behavior, but until you have dealt with your propensity to evaluate God, you have not addressed the root of sin.

The Man Who Overcame

The book of Hebrews records Jesus' victory over the fundamental human issue:

> *In the days of his flesh, Jesus offered up prayers and supplications, with loud cries and tears, to him who was able to save him from death, and he was heard because of his reverence. Although he was a son, he learned obedience through what he suffered. And being made perfect, he became the source of eternal salvation to all who obey him. (Hebrews 5:7–9)*

Why did Jesus offer up prayers "with loud cries and tears" to the one who could save Him? How did Jesus, who was sinless, learn obedience through suffering? And how did this suffering make Him the source of eternal salvation?

The answers are found in Jesus' agonizing intercession in the garden of Gethsemane:

> *And he withdrew from them about a stone's throw, and knelt down and prayed, saying, "Father, if you are willing, remove this cup from me. Nevertheless, not my will, but yours, be done." . . . And being in agony he prayed more earnestly; and his sweat became like great drops of blood falling down to the ground. (Luke 22:41–42, 44)*

Jesus knew His crucifixion was coming, and He went through this wrestle twice.[3] As He considered the agony of what was coming, His human frame recoiled at the thought. We can reword His prayer as an honest conversation, "Father, I am overwhelmed by what is coming.

---

[3]Matthew 26:36–42.

Everything I can perceive in this moment says nails being driven through My body and everything that will accompany it is not a good idea. Can we do it another way?" Jesus' agony was so intense He prayed with drops of blood as He asked a painful question: "Can we do this another way?"

It is not wrong to question God, nor is it wrong to be tempted by our own perception. The issue is our response, and Jesus rejected sin with one statement: *"Nevertheless, not my will, but yours be done."* When Jesus made that statement under incredible duress, He demonstrated His victory over the fundamental human issue. He willingly chose God's wisdom and God's evaluation over His own human perception. He would trust the Father even if it meant His own agony and His own death. In the garden that night, His victory over sin was shown.

Jesus was willing to trust what His Father had said over His own perception even though obedience to His Father would cause Him immense suffering and permanently scar His body.

Thousands of years before, Eve (humanity) lost this same battle when she trusted her perception over God's. Eve lost the battle because she saw something good that God had forbidden, and she did not say *no.* Jesus won this battle when He faced something ghastly and terrifying, but God said *yes.* Everything Jesus could perceive as a man indicated this was an awful idea, but He was willing to put more confidence in what God said even though it required immense suffering.

Unanswered Questions and Unshakable Confidence

God is the Sovereign. He is the Creator. He can do whatever He wants. When creation submits to His wise leadership, everything flourishes. When creatures seek to challenge His rule and usurp Him, it brings chaos and destruction into the created order because God alone has the capacity to rule the created order. There are times God refuses to give us the answers we desperately crave for two simple reasons. First, He will not submit to our evaluation of Him, and second, we cannot grasp His wisdom.

There are times God will answer our accusations against Him with silence to bring hidden issues to the surface and force us to answer a penetrating question, "Do you think you can evaluate Me?" God will force us to answer this question because the serpent's lie still lives deep in our own hearts. We truly believe we can evaluate good and evil, but this lie must be broken. When He confronts this lie, we will submit to His leadership, allow Him to break our humanism, and be healed, or we will cling to our pride and harbor offense.

God does not mind our honest questions or our passionate cries. God does not ignore our emotions, and He does not reject our genuine struggle with things we do not understand. Nor is He unsympathetic to the pain that evil causes. We should not avoid real questions and real pain, but what happens when our questions are unanswered? Do we turn away from Him, or can we find confidence in who He is when we do not grasp what He is doing?

Submission to God is not silence. It does not mean we do not ask agonizing questions. It means we are willing to love and obey Him when He is silent and when He does things we cannot comprehend.

When He was dying, Jesus cried out, *"My God, my God, why have you forsaken me?"*[4] because of what He suffered. Jesus embraced the Father's plan, and it resulted in agony. The cross was an unprecedented moment. Jesus had never been under the Father's judgment. As He bore the weight of sin, He cried out, "Why have You left Me? Where are You?" The words were raw, and the pain was real.

In that moment, Jesus could have embraced offense, but He chose another path. His final words demonstrated the same resolve He expressed in the garden of Gethsemane the night before:

> *Then Jesus, calling out with a loud voice, said, "Father, into your hands I commit my spirit!" And having said this he breathed his last. (Luke 23:46)*

When Jesus felt forsaken by the Father, His response was *trust* instead of *offense*. As the pain of the cross engulfed Him and the cry of *why* came out, He ran *to* the Father. Jesus had passed through Job's crisis and overcome Habakkuk's accusations. He cried out in agony as God crushed Him,[5] but His words were free from accusation. Jesus' trust remained intact when He was overwhelmed by the weight of His circumstances.

---

[4]Matthew 27:46.

[5]Matthew 27:46; Mark 15:34.

Jesus was willing to trust the Father all the way to death. His humanity was overwhelmed, but His confidence was real. Like Eve, He was tempted to evaluate the Father's wisdom, but He was faithful to death. He had an unshakable trust that the Father could bring unforeseen good out of a situation which seemed more horrifying than any of us can comprehend. He knew that suffering in this age is not the end.

Jesus trusted His Father's leadership, though it cost Him His life.

Deny Yourself

Jesus' victory in the garden shows what it means to overcome. Like Him, we will learn obedience by the things we suffer. We do not all suffer the same way, but we all must choose to follow what God has said over what we perceive. This is what it means to deny yourself and take up the cross:

> *Then Jesus told his disciples, "If anyone would come after me, let him deny himself and take up his cross and follow me." (Matthew 16:24)*

Denying yourself is not primarily about suffering or the death you die. To deny yourself means you are willing to deny your own wisdom and choose what God has said over what you can perceive and even what you can understand.

Many are willing to suffer for God because it seems noble. However, God is after something deeper. He does not want you to obey just because His ways seem right to you. He wants you to be willing to deny your own wisdom and choose what He has said over your own perception of a situation. To deny yourself means you are willing to acknowledge your limitations as a creature and trust that whatever He says is ultimately good even if you cannot understand how it is good and even if it violates your perception of what is beneficial.

Until you are willing to deny yourself in this way, you have not overcome the fundamental human sin.

Until this issue is addressed, you will continue to evaluate God according to your own wisdom rather than allow Him to be God and take your place as a creature who must submit to His wisdom. Many believers have obeyed God in costly ways and even suffered, but not yet faced this issue because it is possible to obey God and follow Him at great cost because His ways seem reasonable to you. For example, many believers are tempted by sexual immorality but resist because God's restraints make sense to them. They have seen the negative consequences of immorality, so they agree with God's wisdom in sexuality.

Most believers obey God when His ways make sense to them and overlook His ways when they do not make sense to them. They do not realize this is the fruit of man's original sin. Like Eve, they are evaluating God's commands, keeping the ones that make sense and discarding the ones they do not think are important. We see this constantly when certain sins are warned against (typically sexual sins), but other sins are almost completely ignored (for example, covetousness, pride, and gossip).

God cares about *all* expressions of sin, but we constantly evaluate the list of sins and decide some are greater than others. As a result, we obey some commands, overlook others, and end up living a lukewarm, half-hearted Christianity. This is the Christian version of Eve's sin because we are living according to our evaluation of God's wisdom.

Jesus' answer is simple and straightforward: *Deny yourself and take up your cross. Trust God's wisdom and stop evaluating Him.* Put more confidence in what God has said than in what you believe is right.

When you commit to obey Jesus, you may find yourself pushed to the very brink of sanity where your mind will scream, "This is true, and this is right," and yet God has clearly said something different. Jesus felt this in the garden. When this happens, you *must* choose what God has said and deny what you know, what you feel, even what you think is ethical, and what seems right.

It does not matter what you feel. It does not matter what you think. It does not matter what is reasonable. It does not matter what your previous experience tells you. It does not matter what the "evidence" shows. Human opinions do not matter. You *must* deny your mental capacity to evaluate the best course of action and choose what God has said over everything you can perceive.

The book of Job is shocking and even seems unethical to us because God wants to challenge our evaluations of Him. When you read the book of Job, you cannot comprehend what God does, and God offers no explanations for His behavior in the book. Instead, He demands trust and submission. The reason is simple: *He must break our evaluation of Him.*

If God gave Job reasonable explanations of His behavior, it would feed our ongoing desire to evaluate Him. We desperately want things to make sense, but God will not bow to human desires that began with the serpent's lie and have been shaped by our rebellion. God will boldly confront our humanism because our suspicious response to His leadership is destroying His creation.

Biblical Maturity

Sinless humans can be tempted. Eve was sinless when the serpent came to her. Jesus was sinless and tempted in every way.[6] Temptation is not a sin—sin comes when we respond to temptation by choosing our evaluation of what is good for us over what God has said. Accusation is one of the enemy's primary tools against you. This is so central to his strategy that he is referred to as the accuser.[7]

When temptation comes, the accuser immediately releases accusation in your mind to make you feel unsuccessful. The reason is simple: The more unsuccessful you feel, the less likely you are to keep resisting temptation. Furthermore, when you agree with his accusations against you, it keeps you from approaching God with confidence. No one wants to approach God if they feel condemned and guilty. You must understand his war of accusation against you and how it corresponds with temptation.

For example, imagine a person is home alone and feels a temptation to view pornography. They open their computer and begin to search something out, but they also feel the conviction from the Lord. They now face a conflict: immediate pleasure or obey what the Lord has said? This is not *sin*. This is *temptation*. This person then shuts their computer instead of continuing to pornographic websites.

As soon as the person closes their computer, they are flooded with shame. *Why did I open the computer? Why was I tempted? Why did I almost indulge?* The enemy releases accusations in the mind that make the person feel sinful, guilty, and dirty. If this person agrees with those accusations, they will not run *to* God. They will step away from God, which is the enemy's objective. The enemy wants you to feel like a

---

[6]Hebrews 4:15.

[7]Zechariah 3:1; Revelation 12:10.

failure, like you're rejected by God, so you will not continue to move forward.

But what is heaven's perspective of this event? *Heaven is rejoicing.* Heaven watches this person almost go to the pornographic website, and when they close the computer, the angels exclaim, "Look—they are resisting! They used to keep going without restraint, but now they are choosing God's wisdom over an immediate desire!"

When we face temptation, we can easily feel like a failure. "What is wrong with me? Why do I feel tempted?" Heaven, however, evaluates us very differently. Christian maturity is not a life free of temptation. If there is no temptation, there is no battle. It does not take maturity to resist something that does not tempt you. Christian maturity is being willing to increasingly choose what God has said over what you feel and perceive.

You may be much more successful as a believer than you think if you are increasingly choosing God's wisdom over your own.

Small decisions made day by day will gradually set your heart free from the root of all sin. Over time, the power of temptation will lessen, but temptation itself is not a sin. Do not feel like a failure because you are tempted or drawn to temptation. That is the enemy's accusation. If you fail, it is not over. Seek God's forgiveness, and keep going. Embrace the process. God is full of mercy as you respond to Him.

When babies are born, they do not walk for almost a year even though the ability to walk upright is a fundamental human skill. When a toddler finally tries to walk, it follows a predictable pattern. A toddler will find a stable object, hold it tightly, and use it to pull themselves up. Then they will let go and see if they can stand on their own. When they let go for the first few times, they inevitably fall down. *What happens when they fall down?*

When a toddler trying to walk falls down, their parents pull out their phones, begin taking videos excitedly, and send the videos to everyone they know. They are not concerned the child fell; they are elated because the child is doing something they have not done before. They celebrate wildly even though the child did not succeed because the child is taking steps (literally) in the right direction. They knew the child would walk as long as they persevered.

This is how heaven views you. Keep pulling yourself up. Feel God's delight as you choose His wisdom over your own. Do not be shamed by temptation or a temporary failure. Keep going. Keep resisting human wisdom and the enemy's accusations.

God Is at War with Our Evaluation of Him

God's own name precludes any evaluation of who He is:

> *God said to Moses, "I AM WHO I AM." And he said, "Say this to the people of Israel: 'I AM has sent me to you.'" (Exodus 3:14)*

God is who He is. He is not to be evaluated or examined.

The fall in the garden did not happen because Adam and Eve were guilty of murder, theft, or immorality. The fall happened when Adam and Eve were without sin. They were sinless, but they fell because they decided to evaluate God. God must deal with our evaluation of Him to restore creation and humanity.

God cannot transition this age to the age to come until He breaks the human tendency to evaluate Him.

If God does not deal with this root in our hearts, there is nothing to prevent another rebellion in the age to come. If God saves humanity, ends this age, judges evil, and restores creation but does not deal with our evaluation of Him, then creation could be destroyed again in the future when He does something humans do not agree with. In order to truly transition to the age to come, God must have a people who no longer evaluate Him, a people who trust Him absolutely. This people will be willing to choose what God has said over their own perception of what is good just like Jesus did.

Right now, far too many Christians follow God and obey Him because His ways seem reasonable to them. *They are still evaluating Him.* Our evaluation of God and His ways is the very root of the rebellion, and God is going to tear this root out of His people' hearts to heal the wound of the garden. Now is the time to embrace God's leadership over our daily lives and submit to what He has said even when His ways do not make sense. If we will cooperate with Him now, He will remove this deadly root from our hearts now and liberate us to trust Him fully, and we will be able to stand in the days ahead when He leads history in ways we cannot understand.

If you will submit to God's wisdom in the "small things" of your daily life now, you will be able to stand when "bigger things" come.

God is going to confront the whole earth over this issue, but He wants to confront His people first. His "judgment" (evaluation) will begin with His people before He addresses the world.[8] The prophets were unable to describe in full the events that are coming at the end of the age. Jesus warned that the time will be like no other time, and it must be cut short for anyone to survive.[9] God's end-time judgments will not seem reasonable to us, and it will be difficult to see God's wisdom when the beast[10] takes the stage of history.

If we live through the end of the age, we will ask, "Can there not be another way?" That question is not wrong—Jesus asked it—but God is going to produce a people who say, "Nevertheless, not my will but Yours be done." God is going to use the extreme pressure of the end-time drama to expose and shatter the human propensity to evaluate Him. Before that day comes, there will be many other unexpected pressures in your life that provoke the same questions.

Is your knowledge of God robust enough that you will choose to deny yourself now? What about in the days ahead?

---

[8]1 Peter 4:17.

[9]Matthew 24:22; Mark 13:20.

[10]Also known as the antichrist.

RENEWING THE MIND

Our salvation includes the renewal of our minds to liberate us from the grip of sin. Jesus has given us His mind to set us free from the root of evaluation in our hearts.[1] As our minds are renewed, we are saved and liberated from the sin that grips our hearts so deeply.

The renewal of the mind is needed now more than ever. We have been systematically trained to evaluate everything. We have been taught reality, ethics, and even God can be discovered by humans if they think properly. We are so convinced human thinking can properly evaluate good and evil that we are convinced people will believe the gospel if we present it rationally. We are fully convinced *wrong* thinking is the problem when in fact our problem is *human* thinking.

We can see this in the rampant Christian skepticism that will not embrace clear, biblical teaching unless it "makes sense" to the hearer. We also see it in the common accusations atheists and agnostics make against Christianity. Their accusations against God typically begin with the phrase, "I cannot believe in a God who. . . ." Quite often, this statement is associated with some sort of personal tragedy, their wrestle with the reality of evil, or their disagreement with God's ways. Their complaint is simple: "I have evaluated God and refuse to believe in Him because He does not govern the world according to my expectations." Their complaint is an expression of the root of human sin.

We have forgotten that Christianity and truth are not discovered but revealed.

The human heart *cannot* discover truth and cannot find it by human logic because humans do not have the capacity to evaluate and determine what is true. Truth is not a set of ideas or a collection of ethics. It is not one's moral creed that rules them all. Truth is defined

---

[1]Romans 8:6; Philippians 4:7.

erson not a creed. You cannot separate the definition of good
n the Person of God. For example, God is not love[2] because He
loves" the way we define love. He is love because He defines love.
Love is whatever God does, and good is whatever God says it is.

To renew our minds, we must submit to God as the definition of
good and evil, but our resistance to this is much more engrained than
we realize. So often, we present Christianity as "reasonable." Even
biblical scholarship often falls into the trap of evaluating God when it
seeks to evaluate difficult passages of Scripture through the lens of
"modern ethics." We cannot evaluate what He has said or done and try
to conform that to our understanding of ethics; we must study what
He does and learn ethics from what He does. There are certainly some
passages that are difficult to comprehend, but we cannot let difficult
passages subtly lead us to evaluate God by our "modern ethics."

God *defines* true ethics. We learn ethics from Him. We don't apply
ethics to Him.

*God requires us to submit to what He has revealed because we do not have the
capacity to determine, define, or discover truth with our human faculties.*

When we submit to God, we discover something astonishing: God
does not use revelation to suppress us but to elevate us. God wants to
bring us into an intimate relationship with Him—a relationship that is
so close to Him that He uses marriage as an analogy.[3] God has called
us to become as close to God as we can be without becoming God.
For this relationship to work, we must allow Him alone to be God, and
when we do, He exalts us to rule alongside Him.

Trouble Exposes Faulty Foundations

There is a common saying that persecution makes the Church grow
stronger, but this is not always true. It *can* make the Church grow
stronger, or it can expose faulty foundations and cause people to fall
away. Our understanding of God is shaped by the way we expect Him
to act. When He acts differently from the way we expect, we face a
crisis of belief. Depending on how we respond to the crisis, our faith is
either expanded or challenged to the breaking point.

---

[2] 1 John 4:8.

[3] Ephesians 5:31–32; Revelation 19:7–9.

The vast majority of Christians have not wrestled with God's activity in history.

We can look back on what God has done and often see evidence of His work. But it can be very difficult to perceive what God is doing in the present moment and impossible to anticipate all He will do. The reason is simple: We do not have the capacity to understand His leadership. His goodness is demonstrated *after* He accomplishes His purposes, but His ways are impossible to anticipate fully.

We think we agree with God more than we actually do because the events in the Bible all occurred in the past. We look at the biblical story in hindsight, and we can see God's unfolding plan, but we quickly forget that Habakkuk, Job, and many others did not have that benefit. They could not see what God was doing, and they struggled to make sense of it. Like them, we also struggle to find God in our calamities.

The Holocaust exposes this issue perhaps more than any other event in recent history, and the failure to deal with the Holocaust theologically is one of the great theological crises of the twentieth century. Christians and Jews have interpretations of Israel's calamities in the Bible yet struggle to make sense of the Holocaust because it was so graphic, so raw, and so recent. Even Job is easier for us to digest because we do not have any pictures.

The Jewish philosopher Eliezer Berkovitz compared the Holocaust to Job's experience and wrote, "Undoubtedly, for our generation Auschwitz represents the supreme crisis of faith."[4] No question the Holocaust is a modern-day Job event that goes far beyond the book of Job in scope. Our refusal to wrestle with this "modern-day Job event" is costing us the knowledge of God. We must be able to look into the darkness and find God.

The Holocaust forces an overwhelming question: Where is the God of Israel in Israel's greatest crisis?

Many Jews who survived the Holocaust ended up in atheism and agnosticism because they could not find God in the middle of such suffering. There are no easy answers to the Holocaust, but that is the point. Can you find God when you cannot find easy answers?

---

[4]Eliezer Berkovitz,, "Faith After the Holocaust." In *Essential Essays on Judaism*, edited by David Hazony (Jerusalem: Shalem Press, 2002), 316.

We should be overwhelmed by the Holocaust, and the answers we want may not come, but it is to our shame that we do not ask the questions that must be asked. To this day, we still avoid the painful questions the Holocaust raises about God, and if we are unable to deal with the Holocaust now, how can we expect to comprehend the end-time crisis that will go far beyond the Holocaust?

If you have easy, confident answers to all your questions, you have not wrestled with the knowledge of God.

The Coming Offense

By a plain reading of Scripture, the end of the age is the most tumultuous time on the earth. The Bible tells us that men's hearts will fail them because of fear.

> *"For then there will be great tribulation, such as has not been from the beginning of the world until now, no, and never will be. And if those days had not been cut short, no human being would be saved. But for the sake of the elect those days will be cut short." (Matthew 24:21–22)*

> *"And there will be signs in sun and moon and stars, and on the earth distress of nations in perplexity because of the roaring of the sea and the waves, people fainting with fear and with foreboding of what is coming on the world. For the powers of the heavens will be shaken." (Luke 21:25–26)*

The description of the end-time scenario is challenging enough. However, there is an additional challenge: *God takes responsibility for the crisis of the end times.* Even when the book of Revelation describes the rise of the beast, it puts the beast under God's leadership:

> *And the beast was given a mouth uttering haughty and blasphemous words, and it was allowed to exercise authority for forty-two months. . . . Also it was allowed to make war on the saints and to conquer them. And authority was given it over every tribe and people and language and nation, and all who dwell on earth will worship it, everyone whose name has not been written before the foundation of the world in the book of life of the Lamb who was slain. If anyone has an ear, let him hear: If anyone is to be taken captive, to captivity he goes; if anyone is to be slain with the sword, with the sword must he be slain. Here is a call for the endurance and faith of the saints. (13:5, 7–10)*

God remains in control of the darkest hour of history, just as He was in control of Job's crisis. God will "give" the beast his power. This is a side of God that most of us do not know; we do not know the God who will bring nations crashing down and create the context for a beast to emerge and in the process set the stage for His salvation. Many people are unable to consider a God who sends His judgments to the earth and reigns over the chaos evil creates.

Because we have not wrestled with the way God describes Himself, we have created a "safer" version of God. This is the God preached day by day in many churches. We have created a God who is more palatable to human sensibilities, but in the process, we have reduced Him to a divine being who no longer rules the cosmos to the degree God does. When you form God according to your own understanding rather than dealing with the way He describes Himself, at some point, you are making what the Bible calls an idol. It is difficult to tell at what point our conception of YHWH becomes our idol, but if we avoid what He says about Himself, we are on that path.

God is involved and sovereign in ancient Israel's history and in future end-time events, but we rarely consider God's present and active leadership of the earth *now*. God is much safer, more understandable, and more easily analyzed in the past or the future. As a result, few ask hard questions about God's leadership of the nations in their own generation. However, God wants us to ask these questions. He has given us a record of His activity in Scripture and the prophets' commentary to help us decipher His ways.

God told Habakkuk to "look" and "see" because he could not recognize God's activity in his generation. We suffer from this same prophetic blindness. The proof of it is that we find it easy to apply the principle of God's sovereign judgments through wicked men to ancient Israel and even to the end-time judgments while we struggle to apply this same principle to our present condition.

Crisis, whether personal or global, is a crucible that can either produce an authentic faith in the living God or a disillusioned believer who falls away from their previous confession because they cannot reconcile it with who God actually is.

We must learn to trust and love the God whom we cannot evaluate in the middle of our own situations. It is easy to see God's leadership in David's rejection and flight as a fugitive, but far more difficult to see His love and leadership in our disappointments when we face false accusations and loss. God is preparing a people, not just in their victories, but also in their sufferings, their losses, and their disappointments. Unless we know God in these places, we will not discern what He is doing in the nations and will be unable to trust His sovereign leadership in the storms that are coming ahead.

A Sober Warning about Offense

The book of Hebrews contains a strong warning to hear God's voice and not harden our hearts as the Israelites did in the wilderness:

> *Therefore, as the Holy Spirit says, "Today, if you hear his voice, do not harden your hearts as in the rebellion, on the day of testing in the wilderness, where your fathers put me to the test and saw my works for forty years. Therefore I was provoked with that generation, and said, 'They always go astray in their heart; they have not known my ways.' As I swore in my wrath, 'They shall not enter my rest.'"* . . . *For who were those who heard and yet rebelled? Was it not all those who left Egypt led by Moses? And with whom was he provoked for forty years? Was it not with those who sinned, whose bodies fell in the wilderness? (Hebrews 3:7– 11, 16–17)*

The warning is clear and serious: It is possible to experience the salvation of God and then lose the benefits of that salvation by hardening our hearts as the Israelites did after the exodus. God delivered the Israelites from Egypt spectacularly with unprecedented signs and wonders, but Israel quickly turned to idolatry and began complaining against God. The full exodus story seems perplexing— how did the Israelites so quickly fall away after such a striking deliverance? The answer is simple: *offense and unmet expectations.*

The Israelites expected God to take them directly to the Promised Land and establish them as a nation. When they saw God's power, they expected to become much greater than Egypt had ever been. This expectation was not entirely wrong. God had promised to make them a great nation, but God's leadership confused them. Instead of going into the land of Canaan, God took them into the wilderness, and this delay tested them.[5]

---

[5]Psalm 105:19.

The Israelites could not understand why they were living out in the wilderness camped around a mountain instead of receiving the fullness of their promise.

Israel's unmet expectations caused the nation to embrace idolatry at the base of Mount Sinai. Because they rebelled against God's promise, they ended up wandering in the wilderness for forty years. They lost their inheritance over offense with God's leadership, and this is a serious warning. God may not fulfill our promises the way we expect Him to. If that is the case, can we trust God's leadership, or like the Israelites, will we give way to offense and idolatry?

Many of us assume we would never embrace idolatry, but one of the most common forms of idolatry today is a Christianity that uses the name "Jesus" but defines Him and His ways according to our own expectations. This is precisely what Israel did in the wilderness. They worshipped a golden calf that they named YHWH. They defined God and worshipped Him the way they wanted to.

The message is clear: *We must not harden our hearts over offense with God's leadership.* If we do, we can lose our inheritance just as the Israelites did:

> *But exhort one another every day, as long as it is called "today," that none of you may be hardened by the deceitfulness of sin. For we have come to share in Christ, if indeed we hold our original confidence firm to the end. As it is said, "Today, if you hear his voice, do not harden your hearts as in the rebellion." (Hebrews 3:13–15)*

As the Israelites learned, the words God has spoken will pierce our hearts and expose our thoughts and intentions when He leads us in a way that we do not expect:

> *Let us therefore strive to enter that rest, so that no one may fall by the same sort of disobedience. For the word of God is living and active, sharper than any two-edged sword, piercing to the division of soul and of spirit, of joints and of marrow, and discerning the thoughts and intentions of the heart. (Hebrews 4:11–12)*

Will You Trust the God You Cannot Comprehend

Until we have learned to trust God when He does not make sense, we have not yet learned to trust Him. Habakkuk was told the righteous had to live by their faith.[6] That faith is a trust in the goodness of God, whether He sends a nation into the hands of their "enemy" or He sends His Son to the cross. Only when we come into this level of trust are we truly living by faith.

We must leave our suspicion of God behind. We must form a relationship with God based on who He is and not what we think of His leadership. More often than not, we will see the wisdom of His leadership, but we must be willing to love Him when we cannot understand Him.

We must face this iceberg *today,* or it will sink us when we least expect it. Remember Jesus warned us that the end of the age comes suddenly when men are not ready for it and not prepared, and when it comes, there is no time to prepare.[7]

How can we know that God is good when we cannot comprehend His leadership of history? How can we be confident the God of Job, Habakkuk, and even the God over the Holocaust is ultimately good? What is the biblical basis for that trust? What is the answer? What can save us from offense?

It is time to answer the real question behind these questions.

---

[6]Habakkuk 2:4.

[7]Matthew 24:36–39; 1 Thessalonians 5:3.

THE UNSHAKABLE BASIS OF OUR TRUST

Thus far, we have learned:

- God's leadership can be offensive. He is not always committed to the same things we are committed to.

- Our assumptions about God's leadership can make us blind so we cannot see what God is doing in the earth. Even prophets and wholehearted believers can be blinded by their assumptions.

- God is completely sovereign over history and far more involved than we assume. The pervasive effect of modern humanism and the Enlightenment has perpetuated the idea that man primarily drives the nations and God intervenes when He wants to. This is not a biblical view of reality.

- God's leadership in history is often surprising, shocking, and offensive because He is fully sovereign over evil and even uses it for His purposes. God does not avoid our offense. He confronts it and demands we submit to His wisdom and leadership.

- God requires us to trust His goodness, and He is present with us in our suffering. He hears our cries and welcomes the open expression of our honest emotions. He is not offended by our confusion when we suffer under His leadership.

- The root of all human sin is the desire to evaluate God and His ways. Because human sin destroys His good creation, God is at war with our evaluation of Him. He will not tolerate it, and He will not submit to our reason. Until the root of sin is pulled out of God's people, this age cannot transition to the age to come.

- When we cannot grasp God's leadership, He refuses to explain His leadership for two reasons. First, because we do not have the capacity to understand His governance of history. Second, because He will not submit to our evaluations.

- God demands our absolute trust even when His leadership does not make sense to us.

We have identified a dangerous "iceberg" that is looming before the Church and the nations: *God's leadership*. We have seen God demands our absolute submission to His leadership and expects our full trust even when His leadership is offensive and shocking. God will not (and cannot) explain His ways, but He has given us a profound reason to trust Him even if we pass through the darkest time in history.

We now need to answer the critical question: *How can we trust God when He does things we cannot understand?*

How can a man like Job who loses everything still believe in the goodness of God? How can the people of Israel who have passed through crisis after crisis ever come to the conviction God is good? How will the end-time church who passes through the "time like no other time" and endures the rule of the beast maintain confidence in the goodness of God during the darkest hour of history?

God Himself is the unshakable reason He deserves our absolute and utter confidence. He is the answer to our deepest questions.

God has never offered reasonable explanations for His ways when His people were perplexed, but He has always given the same, unwavering answer to His people's pain: *Himself.*

Because of our rebellion in the garden, we always want to evaluate God. We long for *reasons* to trust Him and have confidence in Him. Deep down, we still question His goodness, especially because we live in a fallen world with immense conflict and suffering. This skeptical way of relating to God is the fruit of the serpent's lie, and that is why God hates it so much. It is a symptom of the painful break in our relationship with God that occurred in the garden, and that break must be healed for our relationship to be fully restored.

Deep relationships must be based on trust and not constant evaluation. Relationships based on skepticism are shallow and tenuous, and this is not the kind of relationship God wants with His people. He does not want a people who appear to love Him deeply but abandon

Him the first time He does something they cannot grasp. This is what happened to God when He brought the Israelites into the wilderness to make covenant with them. Their unmet expectations caused them to abandon God for an idol. *We rarely consider how painful that was for God.*

In order to fully enjoy God, we must allow God to be God and embrace the limitations of being a creature. When we come to this place, God will exalt us in ways we cannot foresee,[1] and we will enjoy an intimacy with Him that eludes us as long as we remain captive to our skepticism.

God's Spectacular Answer to Every Accusation

God has given us a spectacular reason we can trust Him completely at the deepest level regardless of what we live through: *Jesus.*

Any God who would humble Himself to become a creature and then endure the most horrible humiliation and suffering and die to offer life to His own enemies can be trusted implicitly.

> *For while we were still weak, at the right time Christ died for the ungodly. For one will scarcely die for a righteous person—though perhaps for a good person one would dare even to die—but God shows his love for us in that while we were still sinners, Christ died for us. Since, therefore, we have now been justified by his blood, much more shall we be saved by him from the wrath of God. For if while we were enemies we were reconciled to God by the death of his Son, much more, now that we are reconciled, shall we be saved by his life. (Romans 5:6–10)*

God entered into our suffering in the most astonishing way. Jesus bore the wrath of God and the full weight of our sin,[2] and He suffered as no one else has ever suffered.[3] God's wrath is one of the most controversial aspects of His leadership, and God submitted to His own wrath which silences every accusation about His goodness. To say it differently, God's judgments are so perfect that God submitted to His own judgments.

---

[1] 1 Corinthians 2:9; James 1:12.

[2] Isaiah 53:10; Romans 3:25; 5:8–9; 1 John 2:2.

[3] Psalm 22:6–7; Isaiah 52:14; 53:3.

We are so engrossed in our own suffering that we often forget the suffering of God. God has suffered more than anyone. We forget that this entire cosmos was made by Him and for Him. Day by day, He watches as evil destroys the good things He has made. He sees every sin and evil act. He not only sees our pain, He *feels* our pain deeply.[4] God does not require us to suffer alone; He suffers with us.

Humans constantly search for rational answers to their questions. There are questions about personal tragedies. There are questions about the effects of evil across the nations. There are even questions about events recorded for us in the Bible that do not make sense to us. Our questions typically begin with, "How can God be good if . . . ?"

God answers every human question with one, single spectacular answer: *Jesus!* Jesus is the full revelation of God,[5] and He chose to suffer on behalf of His enemies. If this is what God is like, we can trust Him *completely* in everything He does, even when we cannot see His goodness or His actions violate our concept of "goodness."

Some skeptics still demand "rational" reasons to their questions. "How can I trust God when I see evil? Why did that person die tragically? How can I trust a God who claims full power over light and darkness? How can the God of the Bible be good when He judged Israel so severely? How can God be good if the Bible contains stories that seem to violate modern definitions of ethics?"

God's answer to every accusation is the same: "I will not be evaluated. I am your answer. Look into the face of My Son. He is the full revelation of who I am and the answer to every human question. Gaze at His cross and stare into the ocean of My goodness. You can see that I am ultimately self-sacrificing. I suffer on behalf of My enemies. This is who I am all the time. The cross was a unique event, but it was a demonstration of who I always am. I am always self-sacrificing. I always suffer with you. When you grasp what I did on that cross, you can trust what I have done, am doing, and will do in every moment of history."

Many Christians have good intentions, but they offer wrong answers to valid questions. They seek ways to justify what God has

---

[4] Isaiah 42:3; 63:9; Zechariah 2:8; Matthew 25:40, 45; Acts 9:4–5.

[5] 2 Corinthians 4:4–6; Colossians 1:15; Hebrews 1:1–3.

done or compare the ways of biblical wisdom with other philosophical systems. These answers may display elements of God's wisdom, but this is not the answer God has given to our deepest questions. The reason is simple: These kinds of answers are all based on human perceptions of reason developed by fallen human beings, and the human mind cannot come to the revelation of the truth. Truth must be revealed to us.

God cares about our questions, and we must give the world the same answer God has given: *the revelation of God in the Person of Jesus.*

Absolute Confidence

The cross demonstrates the goodness of the mystery of God's leadership. In the cross, God fully walked the same path He calls us to walk:

- The crucifixion was unjust.

- The crucifixion was a profound surprise. No one expected God to prepare His King to rule through suffering, humiliation, and death.

- The crucifixion did not make sense humanly speaking, but the Father required Jesus to trust His leadership.

- The crucifixion caused immense suffering.

- The crucifixion was an evil act that involved betrayal and murder.

- The crucifixion was perpetrated by evil men.

- The crucifixion cost Jesus His life.

- The crucifixion accomplished God's purposes.

- The crucifixion became God's greatest victory.

- The crucifixion brought Jesus unprecedented glory.

Like Habakkuk and Job, Jesus trusted and endured God's sovereignty over evil though He suffered and the wisdom of God was not immediately obvious. The cross is the ultimate demonstration that the evil acts of men are under the sovereignty of God, and if we submit to His leadership, the evil of this age will produce a crown of glory we cannot fully anticipate.

We can trust Jesus. He does not ask us to do something He has not done. He submitted to evil and suffering in this age, and the most evil act in history accomplished the greatest good in history.

The victory of the cross did not erase the evil and pain of the cross. As we have seen, Jesus cried out in His agony. The cross graphically demonstrates the goodness of God's sovereignty over evil without ignoring the reality of evil. It gives us profound hope that God's leadership of our lives is good and will produce something we cannot anticipate even if we experience the darkest hour of human history.

Habakkuk and Job found confidence in the Person of God before the cross. How much more should we trust God?

There are many difficult questions. Many things do not make sense. Many people question the "goodness" of God, but if God was willing to enter our world and die for us when we were His enemies, then He must be good in a way that we cannot fully grasp.

Recovering the Biblical Basis of Discipleship

Many already find themselves in overwhelming situations that have no human answer, and in the days ahead, we will face questions even the prophets of old did not face. We must disciple people before the hour of crisis so they will not be swept away when trouble comes.

Western approaches to discipleship typically emphasize learning. We assume, if people can learn new information, it will produce transformation. Information is important, but it is not the foundation of discipleship. Typically, discipleship is defined by rules and disciplines. Again, these are helpful tools for discipleship, but they are not the basis of discipleship.

Biblical discipleship begins with beholding the beauty of God in the face of Jesus:

> *And we all, with unveiled face, beholding the glory of the Lord, are being transformed into the same image from one degree of glory to another. For this comes from the Lord who is the Spirit. (2 Corinthians 3:18)*

Jesus is the answer to the human heart. The tools we use in discipleship should all be designed to help the human heart gaze at Him, find answers in Him, and then become like Him. New information, new disciplines, and new behaviors are only valuable if they serve the purpose of beholding Jesus and becoming like Him. Christianity is not the only way to reform bad behavior. But it is the only way to behold the beauty of Jesus and become like Him.

We can only trust God if we are convinced He is worthy of trust. Examining His ways is not enough to produce wholehearted trust. After all, He really did send Israel into captivity and led His own Son to execution. If we want to fully trust God, we have to know Him, and if we want to know Him, we must gaze at His beauty in the Person of Jesus. When we get a glimpse of who He really is we will freely give Him all our trust and affection, and the poison of the serpent's lie will be pulled out of our hearts, and our skepticism will end.

When a man is captured by a beautiful woman, he does things he would not ordinarily do. He takes incredible risks and suffers tremendous trials for her sake. He quickly forgets difficulties and trials when he sees her face and enjoys her affection. When we do not gaze at the beauty of God, our trials and difficulties dominate our thinking and our emotions. However, when we are captured by the beauty of God, our troubles become much smaller compared to the beauty of Jesus.

People will endure incredible difficulties and great loss for the sake of love, and it is no different with God. When we really see Him as He is, our hearts will be captured with a love deeper than any other human love. When that love captures our hearts, we will be willing to follow Him into dark places even when it does not make sense.

Though Job struggled with his trial, he was *"blameless and upright, one who feared God and turned away from evil."*[6] Job wrestled with God's leadership, but he survived the wrestle. The secret to Job's success is found in Job 1:

And he would rise early in the morning and offer burnt offerings. . . . Thus Job did continually. (v. 5)

Job was a priestly man. He stood before God on behalf of his family, and he gazed at God's beauty. When God spoke to Ezekiel, He

---

[6] Job 1:1.

included Job in an elite group of men who stood before Him in their generation:[7]

> *Even if these three men, Noah, Daniel, and Job, were in it, they would deliver but their own lives by their righteousness, declares the Lord GOD. (Ezekiel 14:14)*

Take Up Your Cross

Jesus told us to "take up our cross" and follow His path.[8] The command is much more than an invitation to suffering. It is a command to follow God's path even if it leads to death, and to do so with full confidence that God rules over everything in this age and is going to lead us to unanticipated blessing and glory as we submit to His leadership over our lives and over the evil powers that affect us in this age.

Job had to walk the way of the cross. God led Job into suffering just as He led Jesus into suffering. Evil seemed to triumph over Job for a period, just as it seemed to triumph in Jesus' betrayal and death. Job cried out in his suffering just as Jesus cried out to His Father. Job's suffering ended up in an incredible blessing, doubling his possessions,[9] just as Jesus' suffering exalted Him far above any other man.

Habakkuk had to walk the way of the cross. Habakkuk had to put His confidence in what God would do on his behalf, and that included allowing evil to triumph over Habakkuk and his people just as evil "triumphed" over Jesus for a moment.

However, when you follow the way of the cross, the momentary "triumph" of evil produces great reward and unexpected victory. Jesus' resurrection secured our resurrection so we can be joyful and confident. Death is the worst evil men can do to us, and for a Christian, death is the precursor to resurrection.

The cross is God's ultimate demonstration of the mystery of God's will. It is also His ultimate statement of His goodness. He led Jesus into suffering and allowed the evil powers to execute Him, and that very evil act produced incredible glory for Jesus that could not have come any

---

[7]See also Ezekiel 14:20.

[8]Matthew 10:38; 16:24; Mark 8:34; Luke 9:23; 14:27.

[9]Job 42:10.

other way. His leadership of Jesus is the epitome of His leadership of the earth, His leadership of His people, and more specifically, His leadership over your life.

When you read Job, Habakkuk, and—most of all—the story of Jesus, you should hear God ask, "Will you obey and trust Me in suffering, in perplexing situations, in failure, in success? Even if it seems I have allowed evil men to triumph over you so I can give you glory that you cannot now imagine and make you part of My family?"

HE WILL GET WHAT HE WANTS

God's absolute sovereignty over His creation means *He will always get what He wants.* If we obey God, we will experience His blessings and fulfill His purposes. If we resist God, we will suffer the fruit of our sin but *still* fulfill His purposes. God's sovereignty allows creatures to make their own choices for good or for evil. Evil choices can create tremendous carnage, but God never surrenders His ownership of creation. Creation will always ultimately serve the design of its Creator and Owner.

Consider Peter's description of Jesus' crucifixion:

Men of Israel, hear these words: Jesus of Nazareth, a man attested to you by God with mighty works and wonders and signs that God did through him in your midst, as you yourselves know—this Jesus, delivered up according to the definite plan and foreknowledge of God, you crucified and killed by the hands of lawless men. . . . Let all the house of Israel therefore know for certain that God has made him both Lord and Christ, this Jesus whom you crucified. (Acts 2:22–23, 36)

And now, brothers, I know that you acted in ignorance, as did also your rulers. But what God foretold by the mouth of all the prophets, that his Christ would suffer, he thus fulfilled. Repent therefore, and turn back, that your sins may be blotted out. (3:17–19)

Peter boldly called the perpetrators of Jesus' death to repent of their evil. He held them fully accountable for consciously sinning in the killing of Jesus, and then boldly explained that they fulfilled God's purposes *in their sin against Him.* Many people accuse God of being indifferent to evil and aloof from our suffering. As we have seen, God has one thundering answer to these accusations: *Look at the cross.*

In the crucifixion, God graphically demonstrated the mystery of His own sovereignty in His own suffering.

God's most holy purpose was advanced through *His* immense suffering. He submitted to the rage of evil men and wicked powers. He has scars on His body *forever* to demonstrate His own confidence in His sovereignty.

God *personally* endured the mystery of His own control over evil. Jesus was not rescued from evil, but God's all-encompassing sovereignty over evil caused the rage of evil men to exalt Jesus and bring about God's greatest victory.[1]

Jesus is the ultimate example of the way God accomplishes His purposes through His sovereignty over evil. He walked the same path He calls us to walk.

The Pattern of Our Older Brother

Jesus' path to exaltation was shocking, but no one could deny it. He was handed over to the whims of evil men who did their worst to Him, and it resulted in His exaltation. This example gave the early church an unshakable hope in God's sovereignty and His ability to bring about His purposes. If the powers could not destroy Jesus in death, then they knew that *nothing* could derail God's purposes. This certainty fueled the spread of the gospel.

External persecution could not stop God's purposes. In fact, it would likely advance them. Internal compromise and false teachers were serious issues, but they could not stop God's purposes. The early church was unstoppable because they knew "defeat" and "failure" were impossible. They did not put their trust in clever strategies but in the all-encompassing sovereignty of God.

When God handed Jesus over to evil men, it produced unequaled glory for Jesus, and He became the firstborn of a new people who, like Him, would experience degrees of suffering in this age, but also inherit His glory. Paul summarized the early church's conviction in Romans 8.

The suffering we encounter now cannot compare with the glory to come, just as Jesus' suffering cannot be compared to the majesty He has been given:[2]

----

[1] 1 Corinthians 2:8.

[2] Philippians 2:8–1; Revelation 5:6–10.

For I consider that the sufferings of this present time are not worth comparing with the glory that is to be revealed to us. (Romans 8:18)

All things work together for our good. Even if evil men do their worst to us, God will bring forth good just as He used the rage of men to glorify Jesus. We will share in His glory regardless of our experience in this age. God is for us, so our future is secure—there is no one who can challenge Him:

And we know that for those who love God all things work together for good, for those who are called according to his purpose. For those whom he foreknew he also predestined to be conformed to the image of his Son, in order that he might be the firstborn among many brothers. And those whom he predestined he also called, and those whom he called he also justified, and those whom he justified he also glorified. What then shall we say to these things? If God is for us, who can be against us? (Romans 8:28–31)

Paul finished the chapter by reminding the saints that *nothing* can threaten God's purposes. If we experience persecution, disappointment, failure, lack, danger, war, or death, it will not and *cannot* affect His purposes for us. Even if it seems we are like sheep to be slaughtered, nothing can separate us from God's good purposes for us:

Who shall separate us from the love of Christ? Shall tribulation, or distress, or persecution, or famine, or nakedness, or danger, or sword? As it is written, "For your sake we are being killed all the day long; we are regarded as sheep to be slaughtered." No, in all these things we are more than conquerors through him who loved us. For I am sure that neither death nor life, nor angels nor rulers, nor things present nor things to come, nor powers, nor height nor depth, nor anything else in all creation, will be able to separate us from the love of God in Christ Jesus our Lord. (Romans 8:18–39)

We often put confidence in strategies and human wisdom, but Paul put his confidence in God's overriding sovereignty that causes the most evil acts in this age to produce incredible good for His people. Paul had read Habakkuk, and he knew the story of Job. Above all, he knew what God had done for Jesus. Strategy and wisdom are helpful as long as they operate within a biblical paradigm of suffering. There were times

Paul chose to suffer and other times he altered his activity to escape people who wanted to take his life.[3] We should not pursue suffering, danger, persecution, or excitement, but we should live with absolute certainty that everything we experience will advance God's purposes even it looks like defeat in human eyes.

We need the early church's confidence. If we suffer, our suffering will advance God's purposes and, in the mystery of His leadership, will produce glory for us. This way of thinking does not seem rational to modern minds, but it is true, it is biblical, and it fueled the advance of the gospel in the first century.

Perhaps if we thought more biblically about sovereignty, we would rediscover more apostolic boldness.

The apostles could not explain how human rage against Jesus produced salvation, nor could they explain how their own persecution would advance the gospel, but they knew it was true because they had witnessed Jesus' exaltation into the heavens. They had found a hope that was stronger than their fear of suffering. That hope was firmly placed on the Person who is in absolute control of history.

Fuel for Intercession

We can see the apostles' hope in a prayer meeting that occurred shortly after Jesus' ascension:

> *Who through the mouth of our father David, your servant, said by the Holy Spirit, "Why did the Gentiles rage, and the peoples plot in vain? The kings of the earth set themselves, and the rulers were gathered together, against the Lord and against his Anointed'—for truly in this city there were gathered together against your holy servant Jesus, whom you anointed, both Herod and Pontius Pilate, along with the Gentiles and the peoples of Israel, to do whatever your hand and your plan had predestined to take place. And now, Lord, look upon their threats and grant to your servants to continue to speak your word with all boldness, while you stretch out your hand to heal, and signs and wonders are performed through the name of your holy servant Jesus." (Acts 4:25–30)*

This prayer meeting began as a response to persecution, and it shows the apostles' confidence. Wicked men had raged against God

---

[3]Acts 9:23–25; 20:2–2.

and executed Jesus, but it was all in vain because their rage accomplished God's purposes. This gave the apostles confidence to endure their own suffering.

The apostles prayed with passion *and* strength, knowing they could not fail. Even if they endured loss, suffering, persecution, or death at the hands of evil men, because of God's absolute sovereignty, that "loss" would produce incredible glory for them. Paul expressed this hope in Philippians:

> *It is my eager expectation and hope that I will not be at all ashamed, but that with full courage now as always Christ will be honored in my body, whether by life or by death. For to me to live is Christ, and to die is gain. (1:20–21)*

Jesus can be honored by our lives or our deaths, and death works gain for us. Jesus' purposes are unstoppable, and our eternal joy is secure.

Fresh Courage for the Great Commission

Absolute confidence in the God who often brings His greatest victories out of apparent defeat is the fuel of Christian missions.

The Church cannot advance without this apostolic hope. In our time, many are talking about "finishing the task" of carrying the gospel to all people. To fulfill this task, we need fresh confidence in the God who guides history—the God who can use the evil of Babylon, the suffering of God, and the execution of His own Son to accomplish His purposes.

This is necessary to obey the command known as the "Great Commission." Jesus instructed us to make disciples among all people, and He meant *all* people.[4] This includes hard places and difficult situations. It includes loving people that may seem impossible to love. It may include suffering, and some will lose their lives obeying Jesus' command. Obeying this command will not always look successful in this age, but evil men did their worst to Jesus, and it resulted in His exaltation. We are His brothers, and we have the same promise. Even if evil men seem to triumph over us, it will result in our glory and advance God's purposes.

---

[4]Matthew 28:19–20.

If the greatest sin in history (the execution of Jesus) causes the greatest good in history (salvation), then we can be confident God will produce good through whatever we endure.

I fear we still have more confidence in the wisdom and strategies of men than we do in the sovereignty of God. God may deliver you from precarious situations, but He may not. Do you have the absolute confidence that your future is secure and God's purposes will be advanced if He delivers you *or* if He does not?

I fear we are still too confident in our wisdom, cleverness, and human strategies. The God of Habakkuk, Job, and Jesus seems outrageous at first, but when we wrestle with the Scripture and finally realize just who He is, it liberates our hearts. No matter what men or the powers do, He will win which means we will win. This revelation is essential for the end-time missions movement, and once it comes, we will see a forward advance in missions that will eclipse the first century.

The end-time missions movement will be advanced by a people who have discovered the God of Habakkuk—the God who advances His work through tragic decisions of evil men. Without this revelation, we will not have courage to wholeheartedly engage in the task the Lord puts before us. When we do not know the God of Habakkuk, we feel the need to protect ourselves and secure our futures. Our engagement in missions will be timid and cautious. However, when we discover the God of Habakkuk, we can wholeheartedly follow the Lamb wherever He goes.

God is so kind that He gives men the ability to make their own decisions AND ensures those decisions, whether good or evil, ultimately accomplish His purposes.

This does not mean we seek risk or suffering. For example, Paul avoided evil men who wanted to take his life on multiple occasions.[5] It does not mean we should not use wisdom or consider security as we obey God. Suffering is not the goal—unshakable confidence in God's purposes is. The Bible does not tell us to pursue risk or persecution, but it tells us these things cannot thwart God's purposes or threaten our inheritance. We must not minimize the trauma that suffering can cause God's people. This trauma is painful, and the Church should patiently and tenderly minister to those who have suffered because evil can often be *very* evil.

---

[5]Acts 9:23–25; 20:2–3.

God's sovereignty does not erase all the effects of suffering in this age, but our future is entirely secure regardless of what we encounter in this age.

The Ultimate Defeat of Evil

God's absolute sovereignty is the ultimate defeat of evil. Evil creates incredible pain and brings suffering, but evil will accomplish God's purposes and play a part in God's mysterious plan to bring about unanticipated good for His people.

God's ways are mysterious, but His dominion over His creation is absolute. His dominion can offend the mind, but it is the place where our hearts find our hope.

No one could see the glory of Jesus' crucifixion when His tortured body hung on a cross, and it is nearly impossible to see the good God will bring in our own suffering. Usually, we can only see what God is doing *after* He has done it. Our comfort is in a *Person* who controls all creation for His purposes and even makes evil His servant, not in our ability to grasp what He is doing.

We must learn to trust a God we cannot understand.

All Things Are Made for God

We are so easily overwhelmed by our own suffering that we easily forget God has suffered more than anyone else. He suffers in ways we cannot imagine as His good creation is destroyed day by day. He sees it all. He feels it all. No one has suffered more than He has. He even bears the marks of suffering on His own body.

The suffering and evil of this age cause tremendous pain and have catastrophic consequences, but this does not change the fact that all things are still made for God and, therefore, will ultimately accomplish His purposes.

> *For by him all things were created, in heaven and on earth, visible and invisible, whether thrones or dominions or rulers or authorities—all things were created through him and for him. (Colossians 1:16)*

Everything has been created *for Him*. This includes the spiritual rulers and authorities of this age. They can rage against Him and cause tremendous pain, but they cannot change the fact that they were made *for Him*. They will accomplish His purposes. Can you imagine Satan's rage when he discovers everything he has done, including the crucifixion of Jesus and the terror of the beast, has ultimately served God's purposes?

The New Testament church suffered tremendously but understood God's sovereignty so profoundly that they were able to submit to wicked emperors who persecuted and even executed some of their friends:

> *Let every person be subject to the governing authorities. For there is no authority except from God, and those that exist have been instituted by God. (Romans 13:1)*

> *Be subject for the Lord's sake to every human institution, whether it be to the emperor as supreme, or to governors as sent by him to punish those who do evil and to praise those who do good. For this is the will of God, that by doing good you should put to silence the ignorance of foolish people. (1 Peter 2:13–15)*

Peter and Paul instructed believers to obey and respect governmental authority because *all* governmental authority only exists under God's authority. To rebel against government is to rebel against God's sovereignty. Incredibly, these words were written to believers who suffered persecution from the governments they were instructed to obey. These instructions are especially powerful because both Peter and Paul were executed by leaders of the government whom they had instructed the churches to honor.

We can (and must) speak boldly about righteousness and sin, but we must also be confident in what God has said about His own sovereignty. Christians should be careful about people who stir political revolution because that way of thinking rejects what God has plainly spoken about His own authority. We pray and live quiet lives with confidence in the God who leads history.

We must acknowledge our limitations as a creature, and part of this is submitting to what God has revealed about His profound sovereignty over both good and evil as the Creator of *all*. As long as you serve a God you understand, you do not serve the true God. You serve something formed and shaped by your own human mind.

Getting a Divine Perspective
The world is not spinning out of control. Even evil is God's servant.

History is not meaningless. It is being led by a supremely good Person even in our darkest days. From a human perspective, the wickedness of men calls God's sovereignty into question. From God's perspective, we call His sovereignty into question when we doubt His ability to control evil deeds to accomplish His purposes.

God is not concerned with our inability to comprehend what He is doing because we are creatures and not divine. However, He is very concerned with our lack of confidence in His leadership, and He is committed to confronting that.

We should not accuse God of being the initiator of evil,[6] but He has decreed the purposes He wants accomplished, so even when wicked men advance those purposes, there is a sense in which He is the one driving their activity. God takes credit for what is happening in the earth because it serves His purposes, not because He initiates every evil impulse. God's sovereignty over all does not make Him the initiator of evil; it is a statement of His ownership of His creation.

We diminish and belittle God when we believe evil has a power beyond His power.

The reality of God's sovereignty does not remove all the pain in this age, but it does produce confidence and worship. The great saints of history all died without seeing their promises, but they were convinced God would fulfill those promises.[7] Even Habakkuk did not see what God promised. Like these, we must have more confidence in what God has said and revealed than what we see.

Even if we lose our lives because of evil, God can and will do everything He has said He will do.

If you do not look at the world through the lens of God's sovereignty, you will not see what God is doing. You will become blind like Habakkuk was. The end-time church will live through a time unlike any other time in history,[8] and if we do not grasp this lesson now, we are headed for a great calamity. Even now people can be captured by all kinds of "conspiracy theories," but these theories should not trouble

---

[6]James 1:13–15; 1 John 1:5.

[7]Hebrews 11:39.

[8]Jeremiah 30:7; Daniel 12:1; Joel 2:2; Matthew 24:21.

us. Even if there are elements of truth in them, the Lord is still leading the nations, and His purposes will be accomplished.

We all acknowledge God's sovereignty theologically, but often our prayers betray us. How do you pray? Are you confident in the good God who leads history? Or do you desperately "rebuke" every other power and plead for God to get involved as if He is absent and evil is controlling the global agenda?

Evil men may perpetuate evil deeds, but God remains in absolute control. God advances His purpose through partnership with His people, and that partnership begins with prayer, but that partnership must be based on confidence and not panic.

God's leadership is pervasive throughout our lives. He not only leads nations, He also leads individuals. He orchestrates the details of our lives. Things you think are your biggest "problems" could in fact be God's leadership of your life. He could have given you these challenges to produce something in you that would not be produced in any other way.[9]

When our expectations are not met, we frequently harbor offense at others, but what if God is the one who has shaped your circumstances to form something in you?

Joseph suffered because he obeyed God. He was sold as a slave and put into prison on a false accusation, but by the end of his life he did not have any bitterness or offense because he recognized God had led his circumstances for His purposes.[10] Many people want to be "Josephs," but how many want God to lead their life the way He led Joseph's? As we have seen, God also took credit for Job's calamities.[11]

What circumstances in your life are producing bitterness and offense when in fact they could be a design of God to produce something good in your life?[12]

---

[9]This does not mean God approves of heinous acts of evil. God has promised to judge evil, and His judgment will be terrifying.

[10]Genesis 45:5.

[11]Job 1:8–12; 2:3–6; 42:11.

[12]It is important to discern the Lord's work with counsel. For example, this does not mean every woman should stay in a truly abusive situation in the name of God's sovereignty. It does mean that we often are offended at wrongs done to us that are in fact part of God's purpose for our lives.

Exposing Blind Spots

CONFIDENT BLINDNESS

Habakkuk was confident that he understood what God was doing, or at least what God *should* be doing. He never considered that he could be blind, and this is the danger of spiritual blindness. When you are physically blind, you know it, but spiritual blindness is different.

Spiritual blindness is a condition where you think you see, but you do not. Spiritual blindness can be based on ignorance, but it is often caused by unbiblical assumptions. These assumptions often seem right and may use biblical language, but they are not biblical.

If we do not learn the lesson of Habakkuk, Job, and Jesus, we will end up blind and unable to see what God is doing in our lives and in the nations.

We must allow the Bible to lead us to truth and be careful about interpreting it based on our own assumptions or experiences. Jesus cares about this even more than we do. He gave us the gift of the Spirit who will lead us into all truth as we cooperate with Him.[1] The Spirit speaks to us individually and through the operation of His gifts in the Church, which includes biblical teaching.[2]

In this section, we need to examine assumptions that blinded the prophets because they continue to blind us to this day. We need to carefully consider the extent to which these same assumptions continue to blind us and leave us unable to perceive what God is doing.

Like Habakkuk, many of us are not only blind, we are *confident* in our blindness. If we do not address these areas of blindness now, we will end up offended in the days ahead and become subject to fear, anxiety, and anger.

---

[1]John 14:17, 26; 15:26; 16:13.

[2]Romans 12:6–8; 1 Corinthians 12:28; Ephesians 4:11–12.

Habakkuk's Blind Spot

Habakkuk's assumptions produced a massive blind spot that left him unable to see what God was doing in his generation. This blind spot is not unique to Habakkuk—it continues to profoundly affect the Church. That blind spot is nationalism.

Before we address nationalism, we need to remember a few things about how we relate to the nations. First, God uses the nations for His purpose, and He loves the nations.[3]

Second, we are called to honor, pray for, and be obedient to the governmental leaders God has put over us even when those leaders are oppressive. We should seek quiet lives and be exemplary members of the community.[4]

Third, God raises up governmental leaders and removes them. He remains Leader over the nations.[5]

Fourth, there is nothing wrong with celebrating the strengths and diversity found in people groups. God is the source of the redemptive gifts in the nations. He celebrates and loves these gifts, and so should we. In fact, God's desire to form a diverse people from all peoples is part of the mystery of Christ.

With these convictions in mind, we need to examine the issue of nationalism.

Joshua's Surprise

When Israel first entered the Promised Land, the Lord confronted Joshua about this same issue:

> *When Joshua was by Jericho, he lifted up his eyes and looked, and behold, a man was standing before him with his drawn sword in his hand. And Joshua went to him and said to him, "Are you for us, or for our adversaries?" And he said, "No; but I am the commander of the army of the Lord. Now I have come." And Joshua fell on his face to the earth and worshiped and said to him, "What does my lord say to his servant?" (Joshua 5:13–14)*

---

[3]Psalm 2:8; Isaiah 49:6; Malachi 1:11; Matthew 24:14; 28:19–20; John 3:16; Revelation 5:9; 7:9.

[4]1 Timothy 2:1–2.

[5]Daniel 2:21; 4:17, 32; Psalm 75:7; Acts 17:26–27; Romans 13:1–2;.

God miraculously delivered the Israelites and brought them into their land, but before He gave them the land, He gave them this sober message.

When Joshua encountered this majestic messenger, Joshua wanted to know if God would be on Israel's side. The answer was short, firm, and surprising: "No." Israel was a central part of God's plan, but not the center. God was concerned for His own glory. God would help Israel and establish her people in the land, but He was not committed to the success of the state of Israel at all costs. Israel could not assume God would always fight for her and never resist her.

God warned Joshua not to confuse God's glory with Israel's ongoing success. God was in covenant with His people and fully committed to His promises, but His promises would not be accomplished by the success of a political entity—even one formed by the people with whom God had made a covenant. The warning was clear: Do not make assumptions. God can accomplish His purposes in Israel's success *and* Israel's failure.

This encounter was designed to keep Joshua from being blinded by the nationalism that affected Habakkuk.

Exposing the Blind Spot

Habakkuk was shocked to hear God say he was praying against the very thing God was doing. When Habakkuk heard God's response to his complaint, Habakkuk made a second complaint and corrected God *again*. Habakkuk's nationalism was so strong he corrected God before he considered what God had said.

If we read Habakkuk's conversation with God as a story about Habakkuk's blindness, we have missed the point. God told Habakkuk to carefully record their conversation because Habakkuk's blindness is *our* blindness. When we read Habakkuk's story, we are supposed to discover our own blindness and find true sight like Habakkuk did.

Habakkuk was a prophet who truly heard God. As far as we know, he was pursuing the Lord wholeheartedly. He was grieved over the condition of his nation and interceded for it. Habakkuk was a prophetic man and a devoted follower of God, interceding for his community, pained by sin, and longing for revival. *If Habakkuk could be blinded by his assumptions, so can we.*

Habakkuk's nationalism was based on his interpretation of Bible verses. When Habakkuk read the Bible through the lens of his assumptions, he became even more convinced God was committed to Judah's political success and Babylon's immediate demise. He overlooked the full counsel of the Word and could not see what God was doing in his generation. *Again, if Habakkuk could do this, so can we.*

Habakkuk was not the only prophet blinded by nationalism. One of the best-known prophets in the Bible was also blinded by the issue of nationalism. While Habakkuk lived in a time of trouble, this prophet lived in a time of prosperity.

HE SAW THE LORD

The book of Isaiah is one of the most majestic books of the Bible. Isaiah was given weighty predictions about Jesus as God, Servant, Judge, Sacrifice, and Deliverer,[1] and Isaiah's messages are so expansive that his book is often referred to as a "miniature Bible." Isaiah's book begins with several meaningful prophecies, but Isaiah did not see Jesus clearly until he faced a crisis moment that radically reshaped his hopes, dreams, and prophecies.

Isaiah had specific hopes and assumptions that kept him from seeing what God wanted him to see. Like Habakkuk, he was a man of God and a true prophet. He had real insight into God's purposes for Israel and the nations and made incredible predictions. But he could not see clearly until certain assumptions were shattered. Once his eyes were opened, he saw profound revelations about Jesus.

Habakkuk was blinded by his fears, and Isaiah was blinded by his hopes. Both of them had assumptions God had to confront so they could see.

The Death of Hope

Isaiah's crisis moment is found in Isaiah 6 which begins with Isaiah's grief over the death of a king:

> *In the year that King Uzziah died. . . . (Isaiah 6:1)*

To understand this grief, you have to know some history about Uzziah.

When Uzziah became king, Israel was separated into a northern and a southern kingdom, and Uzziah was king of the Southern Kingdom called Judah. Uzziah's father, Amaziah, began his reign over Judah with a powerful military victory but soon ran into problems. His

---

[1]For example, Isaiah 6:1; 9:1–7; 11; 42–53; 63:1–6.

arrogance led him to attack northern Israel, but Israel defeated him, marched through Judah, and took treasures from Jerusalem. King Amaziah was humiliated and eventually killed in a coup. His reign began with great hope but ended in bitter disappointment.

When Uzziah became king, Judah was a small kingdom under threat and probably subservient to the Northern Kingdom. Judah still had the city of Jerusalem, the temple, and David's dynasty, but the people were desperate for hope and longed to recover the glory of David and Solomon's kingdom. Judah needed a deliverer, and Uzziah stepped in to fill that role.

Uzziah was dramatically different from the kings who had preceded him. He was a brilliant ruler. He had several military victories that secured Judah's borders and expanded her territory. He was gifted in agriculture and used this ability to shift Judah's economy. His wife likely came from a priestly family, so he was connected to the priesthood. Uzziah sought the Lord and was taught the fear of the Lord. Uzziah's response to the Lord brought immense prosperity to Judah:

> *And he did what was right in the eyes of the LORD, according to all that his father Amaziah had done. He set himself to seek God in the days of Zechariah, who instructed him in the fear of God, and as long as he sought the LORD, God made him prosper. (2 Chronicles 26:4–5)*

Uzziah quickly became one of the greatest kings Judah had ever seen. Because of his abilities, today he may have been called a "Renaissance man."[2] His leadership ability rivaled Solomon's and filled the tiny kingdom with pride and hope:

> *In Jerusalem he made machines, invented by skillful men, to be on the towers and the corners, to shoot arrows and great stones. And his fame spread far, for he was marvelously helped, till he was strong. (2 Chronicles 26:15)*

Judah finally had a descendent of David who seemed able to exceed the glory of David's reign, but suddenly it all went wrong. At the height of Uzziah's glory, tragedy struck:

---

[2]A person with knowledge, skill, and education in multiple areas.

But when he was strong, he grew proud, to his destruction. (2 Chronicles 26:16)

Uzziah had shown brilliance in war, government, and economy, so he decided to lead the temple as well. Only priests were authorized to burn incense, but Uzziah entered the temple to burn incense as a priest. The priests begged Uzziah to stop, but Uzziah would not be deterred.

The priests reminded him that he was not authorized to burn incense and warned him of the consequences. Angry with the priests, Uzziah took a censor in his hand, and leprosy suddenly broke out on his face. In a moment, the mighty king was humbled, diseased, and disfigured. The priests rushed him out of the temple, and Uzziah had to live the rest of his life in humiliation and isolation. Judah's great hope finished his life as a disfigured recluse.

Uzziah had given Judah hope for the restoration of a kingdom that could exceed Solomon's reign, and some hoped Uzziah could be the promised Messiah. When Uzziah died, it brought a final, crushing end to the expectations for his rule. The savior had failed, and the hope of glory was gone.

Uzziah had not only captivated Judah, he had also captured the prophet Isaiah. Isaiah saw Uzziah seek the fear of the Lord and watched the kingdom transform under his leadership. Like everyone else in Judah, Isaiah hoped Uzziah would restore Judah's greatness as the nation grew in strength and prosperity until the fateful day when Uzziah stepped beyond the boundaries God had appointed for him.

Uzziah was the ultimate king—the savior of the nation. He promised security, prosperity, and hope. He was impressive, greater than any king in recent memory. He promised to restore the nation to greatness and prosperity. He was impressive in every way, his vision of national glory was seductive, and Isaiah had been captured by it.

Isaiah was enamored with Uzziah until his hopes were suddenly shattered.

The Contest of Two Kings

Isaiah's encounter in Isaiah 6 commissioned him for the rest of his prophetic ministry. Prophets typically recount their commissioning at the beginning of their book, but Isaiah's commissioning is found six chapters into the book. Notably, Isaiah recorded this commissioning but did not record the beginning of his prophetic ministry. He was a prophet before Isaiah 6, but the encounter was the beginning of his full prophetic ministry.

Like Habakkuk, Isaiah was a prophet who did not fully see until his encounter in Isaiah 6.

Isaiah began the chapter with a stark contrast between Uzziah and the Lord:

> *In the year that King Uzziah died I saw the Lord sitting upon a throne, high and lifted up; and the train of his robe filled the temple. (Isaiah 6:1)*

Like the rest of Judah, Isaiah had been enamored with Uzziah's greatness. It appeared Judah would be great again—perhaps greater than it had been in the days of Solomon. However, the man who personified the nation's hope was now dead. Isaiah's dream was shattered, and when that dream was buried, *Isaiah saw the Lord.*

Isaiah's vision of God was a vision of Jesus,[3] which means it was a vision of *two human kings.* The first king, Uzziah, had become the hope of Judah, but his dead, leprous body was now in the grave. But there was another King—a *greater* King who was high and lifted up and surrounded by glory.

Uzziah was struck down because he tried to rule in the temple, and then Isaiah saw another King who was enthroned in a temple. One king was not fit to burn incense in the temple in Jerusalem; the other was the central focus of a heavenly temple. The ministers in the temple of Jerusalem warned Uzziah not to enter the holy place, but the ministers in the heavenly temple shook the doorposts with screams of praise in response to the one who was seated in it.

It was a vision of two human kings. One was insufficient; the other was majestic beyond anything Isaiah had ever imagined.

When God confronted Habakkuk, His first command was "look" and "see," and after Uzziah died, Isaiah said, *"I saw the Lord."*

Like Habakkuk, Isaiah had a crisis of vision. Habakkuk's crisis was driven by fear, and Isaiah's crisis was fueled by false hope in nationalistic dreams and human potential, but they were the same crisis. One prophetic man was blinded by his fears, and the other was blinded by fascination.

---

[3]John 12:41.

When Isaiah saw the Lord, his fascination with Uzziah was broken in a moment. He realized the "glory" that had gripped his heart was not true glory. He had been captivated by Uzziah's vision of Judah, but it was a facade. A false hope. Like Habakkuk, he had been blinded by his assumptions and even used Bible verses to support those assumptions.

One vision of Jesus shattered Isaiah's nationalism and infatuation with human potential. Isaiah thought Uzziah was God's human solution, but he suddenly saw a human king different from every other king.

Uzziah had been the ultimate human solution, but he failed. The collapse of Judah's national dream left the prophet and the nation looking for a human solution. The death of the human solution enabled Isaiah to see true grandeur:

Above him stood the seraphim. Each had six wings: with two he covered his face, and with two he covered his feet, and with two he flew. And one called to another and said: "Holy, holy, holy is the Lord of hosts; the whole earth is full of his glory!" And the foundations of the thresholds shook at the voice of him who called, and the house was filled with smoke. (Isaiah 6:2–4)

The first five chapters of Isaiah reveal Isaiah was able to function as a prophetic voice even though he was blinded by his nationalism.[4] This vision began a remarkable transition in Isaiah's ministry. It was the first of many dramatic prophecies Isaiah was given about Jesus, but Isaiah's dream had to die before these visions came.

The Crisis Exposed

Isaiah had celebrated Uzziah's glory in his glory, but now he saw true glory:

And I said: "Woe is me! For I am lost; for I am a man of unclean lips, and I dwell in the midst of a people of unclean lips; for my eyes have seen the King, the Lord of hosts!" (Isaiah 6:5)

---

[4]Some scholars believe the chapters in Isaiah are not arranged chronologically, so the first five chapters are not necessarily the first prophecies given by Isaiah. Regardless of the way Isaiah's book was arranged, it is significant that Isaiah's prophecies are introduced before the commissioning of Isaiah 6.

When Isaiah saw real glory, he cried out, *"I am lost,"* which can also be translated "ruined."[5] It was a raw response to his infatuation with Uzziah and everything Uzziah represented. Isaiah could have said, "I am lost. I have been looking for solutions. I am ruined—I have put hope in things that were unworthy of my hope. I have wasted my attention, my affections, and my time." Isaiah then gave the crushing reason he had been deluded: *"for I am a man."*

Uzziah *had* to fail because he represented the pinnacle of human achievement. He was brilliant and capable. He was the best Judah could produce. Then pride entered his heart, and it created a showdown at the temple. The temple and not the palace was the central focus of Jerusalem because Judah belonged to YHWH and not her kings.

The priests were selected by birth rather than a political process to emphasize God's sovereign leadership over the temple. There was a wall of separation between the priesthood and the king to emphasize the limitations of the king and his government. The king carried great administrative authority, but the nation was ultimately God's. The temple in Jerusalem stood as a statement that there was an uncreated God who guided Judah and the nations of the earth. The nation's future was ultimately in His hands and not the kings'.

Uzziah went past God's limitation and presented himself as the ultimate savior of the nation—a man who could rule the government and the temple. When leprosy broke out on his face, it was a physical manifestation of the corruption in his heart. This corruption was not unique to Uzziah—it is the corruption of the human heart.

Leprosy broke out on his face because he was the face of the nation. The sight of the king gave people hope, and they found pleasure in his royal appearance. Uzziah's sin was a national sin, and the entire nation played a part in the calamity. The nation's obsession with Uzziah had fueled his pride. His ego was Judah's ego. His fall was Judah's fall. Uzziah was a mirror who reflected the true condition of the people.

Uzziah was not worse than any other man. His problem was simple. *He was a man.*

---

[5] For example, the New American Standard Bible, New King James Version, and New International Version.

The temple in Jerusalem was also a reminder of a heavenly temple because it was modeled after a heavenly temple.[6] When Isaiah saw the ultimate temple, he heard terrifying shouts of *"Holy, holy, holy is the Lord of hosts; the whole earth is full of His glory!"* In that temple, Isaiah saw the biggest shock of his life: *There is a Man in the heavenly temple who sits as priest and king.*

There is one Human Priest King who sits enthroned in the heavens. He alone is God's solution to our crisis, and no other human deserves our worship.

Most people think the idea of "worshipping" another human is absurd, but we worship humans more than any other generation. Modern humanism assumes humans can overcome every challenge through discovery, education, and technology. Darwinian ideas present man as the ultimate creature in known creation. In denying the role of any other god, Darwinian evolution makes man the greatest—the "gods" of creation. In our own ways, we have deified man, and it leads to worship.

The essence of worship is the desire to become like another person and in the process give someone else profound influence over us. By this definition, we worship humans more than the ancient world ever did. We idolize people based on the way they look, what they think, the money they possess, and their athletic or artful skill. We adore them, long to be like them, and give them influence over us. Most people today worship celebrities, athletes, businessmen, and other exceptional humans far more than they worship any god—even if they attend religious services. Human "influencers" often have more influence on how money and time are spent than religious convictions, and *this is worship.*

Uzziah was a king who wanted to be a priest. He wanted to rule the temple and the government. He wanted to "ascend" to a place that was not appointed for him. It was a vivid picture of the human condition. When the king who wanted to be a priest died, Isaiah saw a priest who will be King—a man who governs the heavenly temple and the earth. He alone can deliver the nations.

---

[6]Exodus 25:40; 26:30; Hebrews 8:5.

What You Worship You Become

The most prominent sin in the Bible is the sin of idolatry, and in many ways it is the fundamental human sin.[7] God made man to be His "image"[8]—a living manifestation of Himself. Because man was designed to be a living image of Someone he was created to worship, man becomes an image of whatever he worships. (This is foundational to discipleship. For more on this see, the book Discipleship Begins with Beholding.) This is evident in every area of human life because the majority of human learning comes from imitation. Without conscious effect, we automatically imitate what we see, and we are slowly shaped into the image of what we behold.

Whatever you behold is what you will become.

Idolatry is destructive in many ways, but one of the ways it is most destructive is that the idol worshipper becomes like the thing that He worships. Accordingly, the Bible repeatedly warns that those who worship God will become like Him and those who engage in idolatry will become like the idols they worship:

> *All humans have been created to be reflecting beings, and they will reflect whatever they are ultimately committed to, whether the true God or some other object in the created order...we resemble what we revere, either for ruin or restoration....if we worship idols, we will become like the idols, and that likeness will ruin us.*[9]

For example:

> *in various ways Judaism understood that Israel's worship of the golden calf caused them to be transformed and to reflect the calf's unspiritual nature.*[10]

Paul also emphasizes this point in his introduction to Romans:

---

[7] N.T. Wright, *The Day the Revolution Began* (New York: HarperCollins, 2016), 74.

[8] Genesis 1:26; 5:1; 9:6; 1 Corinthians 11:7; 15:47–49; Colossians 3:10; James 3:9.

[9] G. K. Beale, *We Become What we Worship* (Downers Grove: InterVarsity Press), 22, 46.

[10] Beale, *We Become*, 208.

Paul is asserting in Romans 1:21, 23, that "a man becomes like that which he worships."[11]

Isaiah did not worship pagan gods, but his encounter exposed a painful reality. Uzziah had captured Isaiah's gaze, and Isaiah had set his sight on Uzziah as the hope of the nation. As Isaiah beheld Uzziah, he had slowly been transformed into that image. When Uzziah was removed, Isaiah saw another image, and he was shocked. Isaiah's vision revealed he was more like Uzziah and his people than his god. He felt "lost" and "unclean" as he suddenly felt the impact of his political idolatry. Isaiah was not only captured by Uzziah, he had become something.

What images do you behold? That is what you will become.

Unclean Lips

When Isaiah felt the weight of his sin, he cried out, *"I am a man of unclean lips and I dwell among people of unclean lips."* When Isaiah saw the beauty of the God, above everything else he was ashamed of his speech. The reason was simple:

> *"I tell you, on the day of judgment people will give account for every careless word they speak, for by your words you will be justified, and by your words you will be condemned." (Matthew 12:36–37)*

> *"It is not what goes into the mouth that defiles a person, but what comes out of the mouth; this defiles a person." (15:11)*

Our words and our conversation reveal what is hidden inside us. Our words have immense power because they express who we are. Our words reveal our arrogance, our pride, our opinions, our hopes, our ambitions, our evaluations, and our fears. The rhetoric of the people and the leaders reveals the values of a people. In a moment, Isaiah felt the emptiness of his own rhetoric and the rhetoric of those around him. He suddenly felt how empty, arrogant, and ignorant the national discourse was. Isaiah was suddenly overwhelmed by empty words he and others had spoken. Words that celebrated man instead of humility. Words that appealed to national pride and caused division. Until he saw

---

[11] Beale, *We Become*, 208.

the Lord, these words felt powerful, but he now saw how vain these words were.

Isaiah had gotten caught up in the national rhetoric, his lips were unclean, and it had affected his prophetic vision. If Isaiah was going to continue to speak for God, his lips had to be cleansed:

> *Then one of the seraphim flew to me, having in his hand a burning coal that he had taken with tongs from the altar. And he touched my mouth and said: "Behold, this has touched your lips; your guilt is taken away, and your sin atoned for." (Isaiah 6:6–7)*

Isaiah's *lips* had to be cleansed by *fire*. He needed new words. New hopes. New dreams. A new perspective. When his lips were cleansed, his guilt was taken away, and his sin atoned for. Isaiah's unclean words and the nation's rhetoric were not questionable—these words were guilt and sin.

No wonder Paul addressed speech more than any other issue, and James also said our speech is the most difficult thing to control.[12]

We underestimate the effect the discourse in a nation has on us. If we are not careful, our lips become unclean as we engage in conversations and use words that are out of alignment with God's perspective. It defiles our spirits. It is sin. Our errant speech is not a minor thing; it reveals deep issues in our hearts. When we engage in the defiled speech of a nation, it leaves us unable to see.

Who Will Go?

Isaiah had been transformed by the vision of two human kings: One was the best man could do, and the other was the Divine King. After his lips were cleansed, Isaiah heard a penetrating question:

> *And I heard the voice of the Lord saying, "Whom shall I send, and who will go for us?" (Isaiah 6:8)*

Isaiah volunteered, and he was given a difficult message to carry. In context, it was a message confronting the relentless search for a human solution and the futility of nationalistic dreams. Isaiah's message still needs to be carried, but like Isaiah, we need our lips cleansed. We cannot carry Isaiah's message if we are enamored with the empty

---

[12]James 3:2.

solutions of this age. Our speech will remain unclean as long as we get caught up in rhetoric that appeals to the flesh.

The reader should hear the Lord asking painful questions through this encounter: "Who will cleanse their eyes and purify their lips? When will My prophets allow Me to confront their assumptions so they can not only prophesy, but also see who I am and what I am doing? Who will declare My beauty to a generation fascinated by human and political solutions? Who will break free of the political discourse to have a clean, prophetic spirit?"

Tragically, like Isaiah and Habakkuk, many Christians are sincere and have some insight but are blinded by assumptions they defend with Bible verses. The Lord is ready to help us remove our blindness and cleanse our lips.

LONGING FOR A KING

Isaiah saw more than a divine man in a temple. He saw *God's chosen King.* Many Christians assume Jesus is a "spiritual" king but continue to be fascinated by the kings of this age and the empires they build, forgetting that no kingdom in this age will continue into the age to come. Christians who long for human deliverers and political solutions have forgotten that Jesus *is the real King.*

God revealed His Human King to Isaiah, and about eight-hundred years later God publicly revealed His King to the world. The Father sent Jesus into our world as a bold announcement: *"This is My King."* To ensure we did not miss the message, Jesus even died under a sign with "King" written in three languages. Jesus is a *human* king. He is the *real* King who leads a real nation among the nations *right now.*

When we place our hope in any other man, it is both idolatry and a rejection of God's chosen King. Tragically, much of the Church affirms Jesus as King, but their emotions are more deeply stirred by political speeches and national elections than the worship of God's chosen King. We may claim Jesus is King, but our raw reactions to political results, our anxiety and fear over political outcomes, and our willingness to divide the Church for the sake of political gain betray us.

Have we learned the lesson of Habakkuk? When crisis comes, are we filled with anxiety, or do we sit quietly and inquire of the Lord to see if He is leading the nations in ways we did not expect?

When we look to political entities to accomplish what Jesus will accomplish, we are like the Israelites who came to Samuel:

Now appoint for us a king to judge us like all the nations. (1 Samuel 8:5)

Any time we look for hope, salvation, or identity in a human leader or a political entity, God says the same thing to us that He said to Israel:

They have rejected me from being king over them. (1 Samuel 8:7)

Managing Assumptions

Like Habakkuk and Isaiah, we have assumptions about how God should rule the nations. When those assumptions do not come to pass, we tend to blame God, the "devil," or people we disagree with. We also look for human leaders who will produce what we want. When countries rise or fall and things go differently than we expected, we rarely sit in silence and wait for God to speak—but we must.

The crucifixion of Jesus confronts all our expectations about how God should govern and save the earth.

None of us would agree with the cross without the revelation of the Holy Spirit. Paul called the cross "foolishness" to the perishing,[1] and tragically the way of the cross also seems to be "foolish" to many in the Church. But we must remember that God's methods violate human wisdom:

For it is written, "I will destroy the wisdom of the wise, and the discernment of the discerning I will thwart." (1 Corinthians 1:19)

God is not concerned with one nation's political success over another. He directs the nations for the sake of His Son's glory and to produce a companion for His Son. He will bring His people to maturity in unexpected ways. For example, the Lord accomplished His purposes for Israel by bringing an end to Judah's compromised monarchy.

God has not changed. He will do what He has done in the past. The question is will we respond the way the people of God in the past did and become offended with God because of our assumptions, *or* will we adopt a biblical worldview? The prophets beckon us to a biblical worldview. It will not answer all our questions, but it will help us avoid a blindness born of assumptions that may even seem biblical but are in fact not in agreement with God.

---

[1] 1 Corinthians 1:18.

We must let our own personal "Uzziahs" die to see the true King and perceive what He is doing.

It costs us something when our Uzziahs die, but it costs us far more when we allow them to capture our affection and we put our trust in them. It is easy for us to read the stories of Habakkuk, Job, and Isaiah and recognize *their* blindness. However, their stories were written down for us to explore *our* blindness. Like Isaiah, our eyes cannot see, and our lips are unclean. We need a costly cleansing from the fire of the altar so that we may be healed and carry the message the Lord wants carried.

God is looking for human messengers, but first we must see and be cleansed. A fiery coal can be painful, but the heat of that coal can cleanse us if we will allow it to.

When we see our own true condition and the condition of our people, we will respond like Isaiah did:

Then I said, "Here I am! Send me." (Isaiah 6:8)

When a heart is set free, it longs to carry that same freedom to others. If we truly get a glimpse of the King in His beauty, we will cry, "Lord, send me with power to declare His beauty." Other kings will no longer captivate us, and the appeals of nationalism will quickly fade.

Heaven sent Isaiah to carry the message he encountered, but Isaiah was also given a sober warning. People do not always respond to the message. Sometimes, they refuse it, and their blindness increases:

And he said, "Go, and say to this people: 'Keep on hearing, but do not understand; keep on seeing, but do not perceive.' Make the heart of this people dull, and their ears heavy, and blind their eyes; lest they see with their eyes, and hear with their ears, and understand with their hearts, and turn and be healed." Then I said, "How long, O Lord?" And he said: "Until cities lie waste without inhabitant, and houses without people, and the land is a desolate waste." (Isaiah 6:9–11)

Sadly, Israel's blindness increased and intensified, and her people executed Isaiah. The ancient Israelites were no more sinful than we are. If they could be blinded by nationalism and persist in that blindness, so can we.

Like Judah, we are prone to look to political processes for our deliverance. In some places, elections cause charismatic "prophets" to predict great blessing on politicians while Christian leaders get caught up in a frenzy of activity trying to discern and endorse the candidate they believe is "God's man" to secure prosperity. They are convinced God's Kingdom is advanced by the political success of some nations and the failure of others, and they assume God's answer for their nation is increasing power, prosperity, success, and influence. In reality, God brings nations up *and* down for His purposes.

God already has a King, and He has an agenda that is not dependent on the success or failure of any nation—not even Israel.

God Resists the Proud

Israel is the only nation God has ever made covenant with. If God was committed to the success of any nation, it would be Israel, but Jeremiah's preaching contained a shocking revelation: Political or economic success is not always God's agenda for His people.

It is easy for us to look at ancient history through the lens of Scripture and recognize the voice of God in the prophets and the divine work of God in the movement of the nations. It is far harder to have that same confidence that God works in nations in similar ways in our generation. God's work frequently confounded the ancient Israelites, and we are no different.

Ancient Israel did not resist God frequently because she was more wicked than other people; she resisted God because she rejected the way in which God used wicked nations as instruments of discipline. We subconsciously assume people in biblical times lived in a different world than we do, but they faced the same kinds of pressures and challenges we do, and their stories were recorded for our benefit.

We assume God is not as politically involved in the nations as He was in biblical times, but the Bible does not say that. As we have seen, the apostles instructed the Church to submit to all rulers because God remains sovereign over kings. The advent of widespread democracy has not changed this. We tend to think that "we the people" are the ones who select our leaders, but the Bible never says human processes overrule His leadership.

God did not abdicate His sovereignty with the development of modern democratic processes.

Furthermore, God remains committed to breaking our human pride. This pride often manifests itself as confidence that, no matter what challenges we can face, a human solution will emerge. Because of technology and the philosophy of the Enlightenment, humans are more confident than ever that we can "solve" our problems and fulfill our destiny. All our solutions are far more fragile than we think, though. In fact, the simple loss of reliable electricity would render the vast majority of our technology worthless.

God will resist pride in all its expressions, even pride that may be energized and accompanied by Christian rhetoric:

Toward the scorners he is scornful, but to the humble he gives favor. (Proverbs 3:34)

Likewise, you who are younger, be subject to the elders. Clothe yourselves, all of you, with humility toward one another, for "God opposes the proud but gives grace to the humble." (1 Peter 5:5)

But he gives more grace. Therefore it says, "God opposes the proud, but gives grace to the humble." (James 4:6)

Daniel was given profound prophetic predictions of God's ultimate salvation. Daniel longed to see the fulfillment of these predictions, so he asked an angel when this salvation would come. He was given a sober answer:

When the shattering of the power of the holy people comes to an end all these things would be finished. (Daniel 12:7)

This message was about the "holy people," but it is a message for all people. God remains committed to breaking our pride in all its forms—religious, social, national, etc. At times, He will use dramatic events to accomplish this purpose. Many people assume that disasters, calamities, and other events will humble a people and cause them to return to the Lord. This *may* happen. History warns us there is also a tendency to resist God's message in an hour of crisis.

We need to take this warning seriously. We are not "better" people than our fathers.[2]

---

[2]Matthew 23:29–31.

Even Prophets Can Be Blinded

Habakkuk was blinded by his fears. He never anticipated God was leading the political upheaval that frightened him most. Isaiah was blinded by his fascination with success. He never imagined his celebration of Judah's success, and the king's brilliance was keeping him from seeing God's solution.

Habakkuk was blinded by what he feared, and Isaiah was blinded by what he loved. If it could happen to the prophets, it can happen to us. Have you been blinded?

DOES GOD STILL LEAD THE NATIONS?

We reference God's sovereignty occasionally to make sense of the unexplainable, but rarely do we wrestle with its full implications. We agree to God's full sovereignty in theory, but in reality we like to keep the subject of God's full sovereignty safely in the past because it is easier to study the calamities of ancient Israel than it is to consider our present-day situation.

Though we rarely admit it, we quietly assume God no longer interacts with the nations the way He did in the Old Testament. Like Habakkuk, we feel God is distant and remote and worry He is uninvolved in our situation. We have assumptions of what the world should look like, and we beg God to do what we think He would do. Like Habakkuk, our assumptions are usually connected to our personal nationalism.

Because we live in a time of widespread democracy, we tend to believe humans direct the world's affairs unless God intervenes. Few Christians acknowledge this, but it can be seen when elections are held. Christians who succumb to extreme panic in elections related to a candidate or a political party reveal they no longer believe God sets kings in place and removes them.[1]

When Christians exhibit more raw emotion over elections than they do the condition of the local church, it confirms they have succumbed to a humanistic view of the world. God has not abdicated His authority, however. God still rules over the affairs of men whether the ruling class is "chosen" by birth, by a few royal advisors, by war, or by democratic polls.

---

[1] This does not mean Christians should never experience grief over issues in society. We can and should grieve over unrighteousness and injustice. However, there must be a settled confidence that God is leading the nations even when we cannot comprehend what He is doing or do not agree with political policies.

When democracy emerged, God did not surrender the nations to human ambitions. *All the Bible verses still apply in a democratic age:*

"It is I who by my great power and my outstretched arm have made the earth, with the men and animals that are on the earth, and I give it to whomever it seems right to me." (Jeremiah 27:5)

He changes times and seasons; he removes kings and sets up kings; he gives wisdom to the wise and knowledge to those who have understanding. (Daniel 2:21)

All the inhabitants of the earth are accounted as nothing, and he does according to his will among the host of heaven and among the inhabitants of the earth; and none can stay his hand or say to him, "What have you done?" (Daniel 4:35)

Let every person be subject to the governing authorities. For there is no authority except from God, and those that exist have been instituted by God. Therefore whoever resists the authorities resists what God has appointed, and those who resist will incur judgment. (Romans 13:1–2)

Most Christians in democratic nations have succumbed to this idea that human decisions determine the fate of nations and elections. While the ability to vote and petition government is a great gift, human will does not determine the fate of nations. God plainly states *He* sets up kings and takes them down. This includes the "kings" we may not agree with and even the ones who seem to allow evil to prosper.

The idea that humans determine the fate of nations is an unbiblical concept that came from the Enlightenment.

The Enlightenment

The Enlightenment was a philosophical and intellectual movement that grew in strength between the seventeenth and nineteenth centuries. America was a product of the Enlightenment, and the core ideas of the Enlightenment have been propagated throughout the world by the spread of Western culture and the global influence of the United States. The influence of the Enlightenment has become so pervasive that it shapes our paradigm of reality in ways we do not recognize.

Enlightenment thinkers reacted to the abuses of kings who claimed divine authority and proposed that rulers do not derive power from God but from the will of the people. In the process, they deconstructed the biblical view that God was leading history and replaced it with a man-centered proposition. Sadly, this has crept into the Church and produced the idea that God needs to "break in" to history to save the nations. This concept of rule by the will of the people has also contributed to a deep nationalism where Christians seek to advance the Church through political influence and national governments because, if you think history is directed by humans, then you become very concerned about which humans are leading history.

The Enlightenment has deeply shaped the thinking of our time, and we must recognize this influence if we want to recover a biblical worldview. If we do not begin to critically examine the effects of the Enlightenment on our thinking, we will end up with a blindness that keeps us from reading the Scripture correctly and from recognizing God's activity in the nations.

God's sovereignty over the nations is not just part of the past and part of the future. He remains sovereign *now*. There is no biblical justification for the idea God is less involved in the nations in our time. Paul said the exact opposite in the book of Acts:

> *And he made from one man every nation of mankind to live on all the face of the earth, having determined allotted periods and the boundaries of their dwelling place, that they should seek God, and perhaps feel their way toward him and find him. Yet he is actually not far from each one of us, for "In him we live and move and have our being"; as even some of your own poets have said, "For we are indeed his offspring." . . . The times of ignorance God overlooked, but now he commands all people everywhere to repent, because he has fixed a day on which he will judge the world in righteousness by a man whom he has appointed; and of this he has given assurance to all by raising him from the dead. (17:26–28, 30– 31)*

If anything, God is *more* involved in the nations now than He was in the Old Testament period. He commands men *everywhere* (not just Israel) to repent, and He sets national boundaries and sets the seasons on the earth so men will seek for Him. He is still the one who sets up kings and tears them down for His purposes.

When we see disruption, we immediately ask a few questions: How will this affect my freedom? What will happen to my safety? Will this disrupt my culture? Those can be valid questions, but the first question must be, where is the opportunity to reach people with the gospel, and what might God want to do?

Disruption may bring profoundly negative effects; the disruption in Habakkuk's time ended up leading his people into bondage. The crises in our time may create significant political disruption and permanently alter nations.

No matter what the outcome, God sits enthroned, and He still disrupts things so that men will grope for Him. We cannot forget that a sovereign God rules over the affairs of men. He may disrupt things we hold dear to accomplish His purposes, and many of the things we long for are not promised to us in this age. Our response is simple: Engage in the mission He has given us—making disciples among all people—with full confidence that, even if we suffer, it will accomplish His purposes.

We will resist His purposes if we are afraid that His leadership will threaten things we desire, but what if God is not committed to the things we long for?

God Is Not Safe

We have made the subject of God's sovereignty more "safe" by avoiding the full implications of what God has plainly said.

Nearly all believers apply God's sovereignty to the past and particularly His dealings with Israel. Many believers apply it to God's future judgments on the earth during the end times. Very few believers apply it in the present to the same degree.

When we think of our own context and our own situation, we tend to do exactly what Habakkuk did.

We assume that God is orchestrating the nations the way we would. We presume He agrees with our political opinions. We assume our causes are His causes. We are very confident in God's leadership when things seem right to us, but we quickly lose confidence in His leadership when things move in a direction we did not anticipate or do not understand. When we experience unexpected disruptions, we rarely inquire of the Lord and wait for His answer.

We assume we can "see" and never wonder if our assumptions have made us "blind." We rarely ask the question Habakkuk forces us to ask: What if the disruptions we fear most could be God's work?

Habakkuk's perception of his nation and his assumption of what God was doing in his generation were completely different from what God was doing. *We easily forget we serve the same God who sent Israel to Babylon and His own Son to the cross.* Habakkuk could not grasp how God could accomplish His purposes through Judah's failure, and Israel was unable to receive Jesus as Messiah because He chose a path of suffering.

It is possible, even likely, God is leading the nations differently than you think He should.

God's people have often been offended by His ways, but have we considered the full implications of Habakkuk's message? We "see" his blindness when we read Scripture but assume we are not blind. This should unsettle us because we are just as human as Habakkuk was.

We often imagine God's plan of revival will bring economic prosperity and accomplish our nationalistic ambitions. We assume God values our comfort as much as we do and easily forget God brought His Son to maturity through rejection and suffering. Are we willing to trust Him as Jesus did? What if He leads us down a similar path? He never guaranteed us national prosperity or success in various "culture wars."

We often accuse God based on our own wisdom, instead of sitting quietly before Him and asking Him to reveal His wisdom to us. The Bible predicts God will raise up the beast and bring the earth into a time of unparalleled crisis just before Jesus' return. If we cannot trust God's leadership over the nations *now,* what will we do in the days when God brings the nations into an unprecedented crisis? If we are driven to anxiety when a politician we did not favor wins an election, what we will do in the days of real trouble? We have far underestimated how challenging the future will be for the Church.

Many religious leaders in Israel refused to receive Jesus as Messiah because the Father sent Him to the cross. Will we be offended when He allows His people to go through their own "crucifixion" in the end-time crisis? What about the trials you are facing now? Do you harbor offense at His leadership now in the days of small trials?

Many of us are offended with God but confident we will endure the end-time crisis if we live through it. This is an incredible presumption. God warned Jeremiah, if he could not deal with "small" pressures in a peaceful time, he would not survive bigger ones:

"If you have raced with men on foot, and they have wearied you, how will you compete with horses? And if in a safe land you are so trusting, what will you do in the thicket of the Jordan?" (Jeremiah 12:5)

Our God Is Too Small

Like Habakkuk, our view of God is too small. God is just as involved in the earth now as He ever was. He still leads history. He does not change.[2] *All the Bible verses still apply.*

When we do not recognize God's ongoing leadership of the nations, we resist God's right to be God. History is perplexing, but it is not arbitrary.

As C. S. Lewis wrote, God is always good, but He is not safe:

> "Aslan is a lion–the Lion, the great Lion." "Ooh" said Susan. "I'd thought he was a man. Is he–quite safe? I shall feel rather nervous about meeting a lion." ". . . Safe?" said Mr Beaver. ". . . Who said anything about safe? 'Course he isn't safe. But he's good. He's the King, I tell you."[3]

God is not safe, but He is *good,* and He has the power to fully accomplish His good intentions. This should make us an incredibly courageous people.

Reality Is Not What You Think It Is

The prophets did not just predict things; they revealed how God saw reality. If we only read the prophets looking for predictive information, we will miss the main message. Their prophecies were recorded for our benefit so we can know God *as He is.* As Abraham Heschel said:

> Prophecy is not simply the application of timeless standards to particular human situations . . . but a divine understanding of a human situation. Prophecy, then, may be described as exegesis of existence from a divine perspective. Understanding

---

[2] Numbers 23:19; Psalm 102:25–27; 119:89; Isaiah 40:8; Malachi 3:6; 2 Timothy 2:13; Hebrews 13:8; James 1:17.

[3] C.S. Lewis, *The Chronicles of Narnia* (New York: Harper Collins, 1982), 146.

prophecy is an understanding of an understanding rather than an understanding of knowledge; it is exegesis of exegesis. . . .[4]

Our paradigm of reality is shaped by our assumptions, and this creates blind spots because we treat assumptions as truths. These "truths" are like glasses we look through. Those glasses are our "worldview" which shapes our paradigm of reality. As we have seen, those assumptions are often faulty, and God will eventually confront all faulty foundations.

We do not learn most of our worldview in a classroom. We learn it through immersion and imitation by living with our families and in our communities. The culture you are born into is your "world" during your formative years, so we subconsciously assume it accurately reflects reality. Because culture and worldview are primarily taught by immersion, it is very difficult to realize how many of our assumptions about reality have been shaped by our culture. We are all products of our time and our culture far more than we realize.

God Does Not Think Like Us

We are so deeply shaped by our culture we do not recognize that it affects the way we approach everything including God. God does not think like us. God does not share our human cultures and worldview, and as a result we are repeatedly instructed to renew our minds and change our thinking.[5]

God's perspective of reality is very different from ours.

The Holy Spirt has given us the mind of Christ so we can break free from wrong assumptions about reality to know God as He is, but this process requires our active involvement. We have to be willing to let God confront our assumptions and biases that are so deeply embedded in us we never question them.

The primary cultural challenge many readers will face is simple: Most theology in our time is developed and taught from a modern, Western perspective. Because of the influence of Christianity on Western thought, it is also frequently assumed that Western culture *is* biblical culture, but this is not true. The modern Western worldview is

---

[4]Abraham Heschel, *The Prophets* (New York: Harper Perennial Modern Classics, 2001), xxvii.

[5]Romans 12:2; Ephesians 4:22–24; Colossians 1:21–22.

based on assumptions that are very different from the world of the Bible.

Western culture would be very strange to the biblical authors, but because of the immense amount of Bible teaching developed in the Western world, millions of people now read the Bible with modern Western assumptions in mind. Let's take a minute and consider one Western philosophy that has had incredible global influence: the Enlightenment.

Shining Light on the Enlightenment

The Enlightenment philosophy is one of the highest expressions of humanism, and it has shaped the world much more than most people realize. Immanuel Kant summarized the Enlightenment as the courage to define reality through human reason:

> Have the courage to use your own reason—that is the motto of the Enlightenment.[6]

This sentence should immediately be recognizable as the lie from the garden of Eden. *Use your own reason. Evaluate God. Define reality according to your own perceptions.* The Enlightenment is perhaps the most sophisticated and most widespread expression of the fundamental human sin.

Humanism is as old as the garden of Eden, but for thousands of years most humans had some sort of theistic view of the world. The Enlightenment overturned thousands of years of human history by explicitly rejecting divine revelation and constructing a new reality based on human reason alone.

The Enlightenment began in Europe during the era of Western colonialism and was aggressively spread through Western influence in colonialism, education, trade, government, entertainment, science, and other means. The global reach of Western culture after colonialism, largely due to the influence of the United States, has continued to spread the core principles of the Enlightenment through the world. Many of the founding principles of the United States were taken

---

[6]Immanuel Kant, *What is Enlightenment?*, trans. and ed. L. W. Beck (Chicago: University of Chicago Press, 1955), 286.

directly from the Enlightenment, and it can be said that the United States is the greatest student of the Enlightenment.[7]

Many who are religious and even Christian are under the influence of the Enlightenment. Centuries ago, this was typically expressed as Deism, which was the idea that God created the universe and then mostly left it to humans to rule. While Deism has largely died out, many Christians continue to think like deists. They see God as out there somewhere but not intimately involved unless He intervenes.

The Enlightenment has shaped us far more than we realize. A number of its core convictions have become ingrained into us to the point we assume that science can define reality, critical thinking can discover truth, education can solve our problems, democracy can secure freedom, and humanity is progressing. There is value in many of these things, but they cannot secure human flourishing.

In the first century, Paul battled a false philosophy known as gnosticism. It was a system of philosophy built on the idea of secret revelation, and it seemed so similar to Christianity that it became a serious problem. It was a heresy that deeply affected the Church.

The Enlightenment may well be the gnosticism of our time—a dangerous philosophy that can sound right but completely undermines Christianity.

For example, Christians should value using science to serve our communities, and critical thinking, widespread education, and using technology to serve our fellow man. However, none of these things can be allowed to define reality, and none is capable of answering our deepest needs.

The Enlightenment is so pervasive that many view the Bible through the lens of the Enlightenment rather than evaluating the Enlightenment through the lens of the Bible. For example, we assume people can discover biblical truth through critical thinking if the evidence is presented to them, but this is not a biblical idea. Truth must be revealed by the Holy Spirit,[8] and we must choose His revelation over our own logic.

The assumptions of the Enlightenment create blind spots when we read the Bible because the Bible directly opposes the philosophical

---

[7]Stuart Greaves, personal conversation.

[8]Romans 8:7–8; 2 Corinthians 4:4; Ephesians 2:1; 4:17–19; Galatians 4:8; Colossians 1:21; 2:13; 1 John 2:11.

foundation of the Enlightenment. We can never discover the knowledge of God when we read the Bible through a lens shaped by people who either believe God does not exist or that, if He does, He must be defined by modern, humanistic ideas.

Turning Out the Lights on the Enlightenment

People assume the incredible increase in information, scientific discoveries, and the advance of technology validate the premises of the Enlightenment, but this is not true. The Enlightenment is a worldview just like any other worldview, and it was built on a faulty foundation. It is easy to forget that the Enlightenment is only a few hundred years old, and the vast majority of humans who have lived viewed the world very differently. While we tend to think we are more advanced than previous generations, the idea that our thinking is superior to most of humanity is incredibly arrogant.[9]

If you have been immersed in Enlightenment thinking, and most of us have been, then you look at reality in a way that seems to validate the Enlightenment, but this will change. If you look at the world through the "glasses" of the Enlightenment, current events seem to validate its assumptions. When you take these glasses off, you discover the hope of the Enlightenment is an illusion.

In the days ahead, God will expose the false foundations of the Enlightenment, and it will collapse. The Enlightenment made incredible promises about the future of humanity, and it simply cannot keep those promises. Education, science, and technology are useful tools, but they cannot bring about a utopia, they cannot make man flourish, and they cannot solve the fundamental human issues.

God is committed to exposing the arrogance of man and the limitation of human wisdom, so He will expose the Enlightenment, and it will collapse on its own faulty foundations.

The worldview the Enlightenment defined feels natural to us, but it is a facade. In the days ahead, we will view the Enlightenment the way we now view the mythology of the ancient Greeks. It will be a system of thought that ran its course and was incapable of saving humankind.

The world still operates based on many of the Enlightenment's assumptions. Progress is assumed. Technology is central. Science

---

[9]Especially considering how many ancient accomplishments remain mystifying to us.

defines truth. Human reason can solve all problems. This is the way people view reality, but it is not real. Reality is not defined by human progress; it is determined by the sovereign actions of an intricately involved God who is leading history to His ends. The spiritual component of our world is much greater than the philosophers have acknowledged, and this will be apparent in the days ahead.

Right now, people remain fixated on the promise of technology, progress, science, and education. While these are good things in their proper context, they are not ultimate. The truth will be revealed, and we will see that the world is not complete the way the Enlightenment had defined it. Things society now assumes are true will be exposed as vain imaginations.

The fall of the Enlightenment will create a crisis we have not anticipated. There will be a profound panic because people need some sort of framework for reality. People will desperately look for something to fill the void and offer new answers to humanity's deepest questions.[10]

The world is growing more religious, not less, and this will accelerate as the Enlightenment unravels.[11] Very few are anticipating the collapse of the Enlightenment, but it is coming. When it collapses, the world is going to be confronted by the God of Habakkuk.

---

[10]If we are close to the Lord's return, it is very possible that the man often called the "beast" (antichrist) will fill the vacuum that follows the failure of the Enlightenment with a new philosophy and a new worldview. The failure of the Enlightenment could provide a moment for a rapid transition to a new philosophy even darker than the one it replaces.

[11]Noah Rayman, "The World Is Getting More Religious," *Time*, April 2, 2015, https://time.com/3769287/religion-atheists-study/.

LEARNING GOD'S WAYS

Because God is intensely relational,[1] He reveals Himself through what He does and how He relates. As a result, most of the Bible consists of stories that reveal God's character through His actions and His relationships with His people. When we study the events of the Bible, past and predicted, we are not primarily studying events. We are discovering a Person. Our expectations concerning God's behavior are part of our knowledge of God, and if our knowledge of God is not true, our foundation is faulty.

We should not read the Bible as a history book. It was not written principally to tell us what happened in the past; it was written to reveal who God is so we can understand His activity in our lives.

The Bible describes certain patterns in God's judgment we must know. These patterns predominantly apply to Israel, but they reveal how God relates to man and can help us recognize what God is doing.

God is abundantly merciful and patient, so He will wait a lengthy period of time before He judges. Because He is so patient, we could assume He is uninvolved, He does not care, or we are in a better condition than we really are. Depending on our perspective, we often either accuse God of not caring or become comfortable in our compromise because we do not see an immediate judgment.

God's patience over decades, and sometimes generations, can lead us to assume He is pleased with things He is not pleased with. We can also assume that God wants something to continue when in reality He is directly opposed to it. When we merge these assumptions with Bible verses, we develop convictions about how God thinks about His people and the nations. These convictions form a faulty foundation, and soon we become convinced God is committed to things He is not

---

[1] The Trinity reveals God dwells in community in a way we cannot grasp.

committed to, or He approves of things He does not approve of because of His patience and long-suffering.

In reality, God's patience toward His people and toward nations is not an endorsement; it expresses His desire for repentance:

> The Lord is . . . patient toward you, not wishing that any should perish, but that all should reach repentance. (2 Peter 3:9)

If we live in a time of peace, we are especially susceptible to this fault because we prefer comfort and want our times of peace to continue.

When God is ready to judge, He may release warnings over decades. When "storm clouds" begin gathering on the horizon, people often ignore them and suppose they will go away, so when God releases His judgments, they often come as a complete shock. When God strikes a nation and then allows it to return to "normal," it is an act of mercy designed to produce repentance. God will disrupt us so we consider our ways because crisis can shake us out of our daily delusions. People in crisis ask much more serious questions than they do in times of peace.

When God removes the intensity of His judgment, He looks to see how we will respond. As life feels more "normal," do we take advantage of the calm to respond to the Lord, or do we quickly return to our old ways revealing that any change was superficial?

There is an old saying, "There are no atheists in foxholes"; however, there are many who survive the foxholes and quickly forget their cries to God.

The calm after a crisis is very important because it is a gift from the Lord *and* a test. He looks to see how men respond when the pressure is lifted. Was their repentance in the moment of duress real? Do they truly want to change their ways? Regrettably, most do not change. This revelation can also happen when a crisis continues for a lengthy period of time. When it begins, people feel a panic, but as a crisis endures, people find a "new normal," and their old ways begin to re-emerge if they have not truly repented.

God delays judgment because He longs to give mercy, but delayed judgment also emboldens people in their sin.

God will often bring cycles of judgment and calm to produce repentance or show a lack of repentance. These cycles typically unfold over many decades. Many people read the story of ancient Israel and wonder why Israel did not respond to the Lord's judgments, but one reason was that the judgments unfolded over decades even though the stories can be read in a few hours. If we do not recognize these patterns, we will presume the trouble is always "from the enemy" and not from the Lord when it may be the Lord. Furthermore, we will imagine peace is an indicator of the Lord's favor when it could be the Lord evaluating a people under judgment.

Recognizing God's Leadership

Habakkuk's complaint was a familiar one, "God, You are not involved and have not answered my prayers." That was his first crisis. Once Habakkuk found out that God was active, he faced a second, larger crisis of faith: He did not agree with God's leadership.

We often define God's goodness within a framework of how we understand goodness. We hesitate to declare that EVERYTHING He does in the nations is good.

God's leadership over the nations is one of the greatest challenges the Church will face in the years ahead, particularly in affluent, Western nations. The Western world has experienced unprecedented peace, prosperity, safety, and freedom in the last fifty years. Many Western countries have some degree of Christian influence in their cultures, and many Western Christians believe Western prosperity is connected to their culture's often superficial acknowledgment of some Christian values.

This mixture of Western values with Christianity has produced the presumption that God's primary goal is to preserve the wealth, peace, and comfort of the Western world. As a result, Western Christians typically believe God is committed to modern, Western culture and even assume their nations are connected to the Kingdom of God in some way. This idea has been prevalent throughout the history of the West and remains common in the United States.

We quickly forget the conversation Joshua had with an angel before Israel went into the Promised Land:

When Joshua was by Jericho, he lifted up his eyes and looked, and behold, a man was standing before him with his drawn sword in his hand. And Joshua went to him and said to him, "Are you for us, or for our adversaries?" And he said, "No; but I am the commander of the army of the LORD. Now I have come." And Joshua fell on his face to the earth and worshiped and said to him, "What does my lord say to his servant?" (Joshua 5:13–14)

God's message to Joshua is a message to every believer. In our time, we could ask, "Are You for America or for China?" The Lord's answer would be the same. "Neither." God does not need America or China to prosper, fail, or even survive to accomplish His objectives. If this statement sounds shocking, it exposes the fact that we have confused our nations with His Kingdom. God uses the nations for His purposes, and those purposes are focused on a different Kingdom.

There is a pattern of blessing at some level when people follow God's ways, but this principle has been grossly misinterpreted to the point that we believe God's primary goal is to restore affluence and comfort if people will simply pray a few prayers of repentance, obey a few biblical injunctions, and give God token acknowledgment. Many Christians assume God is fully committed to their nation's affluence and global leadership. These are cultural assumptions but not biblical ones. If we look at the world this way, it will blind us to God's activity.

God raises nations up and brings them down according to His purpose. *Every* nation's foundation is faulty, and God is not committed to the permanent success of any nation, not even ones many believe are "Christian."[2] He uses *all* nations for His purposes. Our part is simply to live with confidence in His leadership as good citizens wherever He has placed us.

Is God Committed to What You Are Committed To?

Sermons and popular books reveal wrong assumptions. We have endless books, sermons, and conferences on how living by God's principles will bring greater happiness and prosperity in this age, but this is a pagan approach to God. Ancient pagans served their gods to obtain blessing, and when we present Jesus the same way, it is dangerously close to witchcraft. We search for biblical "spells" to achieve our desired outcomes. In the process, God becomes a means to our desired ends.

---

[2]While some nations have more Christian cultural influences, the concept of a truly "Christian nation" is not a biblical one. According to the New Testament, there is only one Christian nation—the Church.

We rarely soberly consider the fact that the New Testament presents suffering as a gift:

For it has been granted to you that for the sake of Christ you should not only believe in him but also suffer for his sake. (Philippians 1:29)

Nor do we consider that the New Testament promises suffering and does not promise wealth or comfort in this age. Some believers will experience wealth and comfort, but this is abnormal based on the New Testament. We are inspired by those who suffer but rarely consider if we should suffer. When we lose freedoms or experience pressure for our faith, do we escalate "cultural wars" or thoughtfully ask if the Lord is the one who is leading us into suffering? We should not compromise our faith, but when pressure comes, we must ask if He is the one leading us to suffer, endure, and honor the very authorities placed over us as the New Testament church did.

For example, American Christians are very concerned about certain cultural trends, and they should be—the Church will need wisdom to navigate these trends. However, if you read Habakkuk thoughtfully and carefully, it requires you to ask a very solemn question about America:[3] Is it possible God is the one who has stirred up some of the cultural trends American Christians are most terrified of? Could He be intricately involved in trends that many Christians assume are nothing more than evil attacks on Christian values? Could He be forming something in His people that cannot come another way?

While many of the cultural trends in America are challenging for the Church, they have also broken the facade of nominal cultural Christianity that has been present throughout much of America's history. Biblically, God is not committed to America, or any other political structure, becoming His people. He has one Nation, the Church, and He directs all of history for the good of that Nation. As we have seen, He directs history differently than we would. It is possible the pressure of the culture may force American Christians to ask serious questions that could result in a more biblical Christianity and a more committed Church as the culture rejects certain Christian norms. If we take the Bible seriously, we must ask these kinds of questions.

---

[3]America is just an example. Of course this applies to other nations as well.

Many American readers will read this, immediately think of a cultural issue and say, "This cultural trend is clearly unbiblical, so God cannot possibly be involved. He must want us to turn the culture." *This is exactly what Habakkuk thought.* Our inability to consider if God is involved in shifting cultural trends that threaten our idea of a "moral" nation reveal we have not wrestled with Habakkuk's message. We *must* carefully consider how many of our opinions come from Bible verses and how many are seemingly reasonable assumptions not actually based on Bible verses.

Babylon was a wicked, immoral nation, which is precisely why God's message to Habakkuk was so challenging. God agreed with Habakkuk about Babylon's condition and never asked Habakkuk to agree with their wickedness. God does not ask us to affirm and celebrate unbiblical cultural trends. However, just as God used Babylon to advance His purposes for Israel, based on Bible verses, God will use cultural trends to accomplish His purposes for His Church—even trends that may seem unbiblical. We will not always see what God is doing, but we must have unshakable confidence in His leadership.

God's goal is to secure our present holiness for our eternal happiness rather than to secure our present comfort for our temporal happiness.

Many agree God is focused on our eternal happiness but do not live as if it is true, and this creates blindness. Ancient Judah assumed God was fully committed to Israel's prosperity and strength. Judah worshiped God primarily for the benefits He would give and was convinced any pressure she faced came from "enemies" and not from God, but she was wrong. We have many of the same convictions Judah had. We assume power and prosperity will come if nations embrace certain biblical values. Could we be blind as well?

When we succumb to blindness, we view the world politically and assume this age is a conflict between "good" nations and "bad" nations. While some nations are *functionally* superior to others, none is *morally* superior to others. Some governmental systems provide a better framework for quality of life, but every nation is ultimately an unrighteous nation by God's standards. God is building His own

Kingdom, and that Kingdom does not depend on any nation in this age. It transcends them *all*.[4]

Could we be blind like Habakkuk? Could we be approaching a hidden iceberg like the Titanic?

---

[4]No nation in this age is the "Kingdom of God," whether it be nations with a semblance of Christian culture, like America, or the Modern State of Israel. The State of Israel is part of God's ongoing and unique pursuit of the Jewish people, but it is an unrighteous state and not the final fulfillment of God's promises to the Jewish people.

Becoming a People Who Can See

There are many things that contribute to blindness among Christians. The more obvious things include embracing sin, wrong interpretations of Scripture, and refusal to obey Scripture. Nationalism is also one of the biggest sources of Christian blindness, and it is particularly dangerous because it often goes undetected. Nationalism fueled by wrong assumptions and incorrect interpretations of Scripture brings a "blindness" that leaves us unable to see what God is doing. This blindness can affect individuals who genuinely love God, including prophets, and people often use Scripture out of context to promote it.

There are two things necessary to avoid the trap of nationalism. *First, we must have full confidence in God's leadership of history, especially when we cannot understand what He is doing.* God leads history very differently than we would. He can use our suffering as easily as He can use our success. Because we do not always comprehend His leadership, we must have unshakable confidence that God will produce good even if it seems evil has triumphed.

Evil cannot derail God's purposes, and His leadership is so all-encompassing that evil ends up advancing His purposes. This does not make God the author of evil, it does not minimize the trauma of evil, and God will still hold the wicked accountable for their deeds. We have dealt with this issue extensively because it has the potential to produce offense in God's people. Now, we must turn to the second thing necessary.

Second, to avoid nationalism and the subsequent blindness that follows, we must know that the Church is a nation—a real nation.[1] In fact, the nature and identity of the Church as a nation is essential to understanding the

---

[1] I am especially grateful to Stuart Greaves for long conversations on this subject and have learned much from his clarity on the nature of the church.

gospel. Many believers are unaware of just how significant this aspect of the Church's identity is, but the New Testament clearly presents the Church as a nation:

> *Therefore, we are ambassadors for Christ, God making his appeal through us. (2 Corinthians 5:20)*

> *You are no longer strangers and aliens, but you are fellow citizens with the saints and members of the household of God. (Ephesians 2:19)*

> *Praying at all times in the Spirit . . . making supplication for all the saints, and also for me, that words may be given to me in opening my mouth boldly to proclaim the mystery of the gospel, for which I am an ambassador in chains, that I may declare it boldly, as I ought to speak. (6:18–20)*

> *But our citizenship is in heaven, and from it we await a Savior, the Lord Jesus Christ. (Philippians 3:20)*

> *But you are a chosen race, a royal priesthood, a holy nation, a people for his own possession, that you may proclaim the excellencies of him who called you out of darkness into his marvelous light. (1 Peter 2:9)*

> *To him who loves us and has freed us from our sins by his blood and made us a kingdom. . . . (Revelation 1:5–6)*

These verses are familiar to many Christians, but consider the words in these verses: *ambassadors, citizens, nation, kingdom.* Imagine you are hearing these words for the first time. The language is clear. The Church is not just a spiritual family; it is a nation among the nations. We live in exile in this age waiting for our King to return.

The apostles viewed the Church as a real nation, and so did the Romans. The Roman persecution of Christianity was fueled in part by political concerns. The early Christians were model citizens, but Roman rulers were insecure and threatened by the preaching of Jesus as King.[2] To overcome nationalism, we need to see the Church as a nation and learn how the Bible instructs us to relate to the nations of this age.

---

[2] Acts 17:6–7.

Words Matter

We need to understand the way the New Testament uses the word *nation* so that we avoid some common mistakes. The word typically translated "nation" in English New Testament is "*ethnos*" (ἔθνος),[3] and it refers to people groups not political entities. The word was typically used to refer to gentile people groups. The current emphasis in the Church to reach all "people groups" was based in part on correcting the false notion that *ethnos* meant political entities instead of peoples. Missiologists correctly realized it is not enough to have a church in every political entity; God wants churches among every people group.

Even though this issue has been widely discussed in the Church since the mid 1970s, people continue to assume the word *nation* means political entities, and as a result incredible amounts of time and resources continue to be invested in causes that the New Testament does not call us to take up.

Let's consider two verses where the use of *ethnos* is significant. First, in Matthew 24, Jesus warned His followers about conflict between the nations:

For nation will rise against nation. . . . (v. 7)

In context, this is a warning about racial and ethnic tension, not political conflict. (Jesus warned about political strife in the second half of the verse.) Jesus focused our attention on racial and ethnic conflict so the Church would be a demonstration of racial and ethnic unity and work to heal this kind of conflict. Many people have overlooked Jesus' instruction by assuming "nation" here meant conflict between political states, but we need to heed this warning and be deeply concerned about addressing issues of racial conflict. The Church should present God's solution to racial conflict: a corporate people who are very diverse and live in unity with demonstrable love for one another. In His great prayer, Jesus identified this as the primary demonstration of the gospel in this age.[4] (Can we honestly say our churches see the glory of

---

[3] For example, see Matthew 24:7; 28:19; Mark 13:8; Luke 21:10; 23:2; John 11:48, 50; Acts 7:7.

[4] John 17:21, 23.

"one new man" living in love and unity as the principal proof of the gospel?)

Second, in Matthew 28, Jesus instructed the Church to make disciples of all nations:

> *Go therefore and make disciples of all nations, baptizing them in the name of the Father and of the Son and of the Holy Spirit. (Matthew 28:19)*

This is not a command to disciple political states but an instruction to make disciples among all people groups. This command is an expression of God's love and desire for a people from all peoples. The idea of "discipling" political states does not even make sense because organizations cannot be discipled—only people can. Because this verse has been misinterpreted, an incredible amount of energy has been spent trying to determine what it takes to "disciple" political states even though Jesus never asked us to do this. Likewise, the apostles never tried to "disciple" political structures, nor did they teach the Church to do this, but many Christians have spent a lot of energy on this and justified it in part based on a wrong interpretation of the English translation of *ethnos*. Jesus did not commission us to save the nations but to proclaim the good news of His Kingdom—His Nation.

Every follower of Jesus should be an influence for good and represent the gospel wherever the Lord has put them, but there is not a single verse in the New Testament instructing us to seek political, societal, or governmental influence as a missional strategy. The New Testament does not teach us to accomplish the Great Commission through the structures of this age which include political and governmental structures.

God *loves* the nations (peoples) of the earth, but He is not committed to the political structures of this age. Habakkuk and Isaiah confused the two, and this confusion remains rampant in many parts of the Church. We must address this issue, or we will be blind and unable to see what God is doing. If we do not address it, there are serious consequences. We can become fearful, anxious, and offended while praying for things that are in fact the opposite of what God is actually doing. We can also become proud and celebrate things that God does not celebrate and is not committed to.

We are instructed to respect the political structures in this age (without violating God's commands), pray for leaders, and seek to live quiet lives advancing the gospel.[5] While God uses the nations for His purposes, our part is to advance the gospel through discipling people groups in the context of the Church, not attempting to advance the gospel by aligning it with political causes. Nor should we allow ambitious politicians to use the Church to achieve their political objectives.

A Nation in Exile

The Bible is clear that none of the political entities in this age will survive into the age to come—not even the one called "Israel."[6] The concept of "sheep" and "goat" nations often drawn from Jesus' judgment in Matthew 25[7] is not biblical:

> *Before him will be gathered all the nations [people groups], and he will separate people one from another as a shepherd separates the sheep from the goats. (v. 32)*

Jesus predicted He will gather people groups (*ethnos*) for judgment, not political entities. Then He will separate people from these people groups. Jesus will gather the "sheep" and "goats" out of all people groups; He will not designate some nation states as "sheep" and others as "goats."

God leads the nations for His purposes in this age, and His purposes can be summarized by two objectives: He wants to reveal Himself through His Son, and He wants to form a people for His Son. It is easy to look around the nations and wonder which one God is "for," but this is not a biblical worldview. The nations of the earth ultimately serve His purposes related to the formation of the Church

---

[5] 1 Timothy 2:1–2.

[6] Psalm 2:1–9; Isaiah 11:10–16; 13:8; 24:1, 4–6; 27:12–13; 34:1–8; 35:4; 42:6–24; 49:5–25; 61:1–2; 63:1–6; Jeremiah 30:3–24; 31:1–23; 51:6; Ezekiel 20:33–44; 36:3, 5–7, 9, 15; 39:25–29; Daniel 2:44; 7:13–14, 21–22; 12:1; Hosea 11:10–11; Amos 5:18–20; 9:8–15; Joel 2:6; 3:1–4, 11–17; Zephaniah 3:19–20; Zechariah 9:10–14; 12:2–3; 13:8–9; 14:1–4, 9; Matthew 24:21–22; Revelation 19:15–16.

[7] Matthew 25:31–46.

who is His eternal companion. God will not hesitate to raise nations up or bring them down if it serves His purposes for His Church.

We frequently reduce the Church to a "spiritual kingdom," but it is much more than that. It is a real kingdom ("nation" in modern language) among the nations. Jesus died under a sign that said *"King of the Jews"* in three languages. It did not say Savior or Servant though He is both. When Jesus died, He died as a king, and when He ascended, He began gathering people into a nation under His leadership. We are citizens and ambassadors of that Nation.

Jesus' first sermon began with, *"Repent, for the kingdom of heaven is at hand."*[8] He sent the apostles to speak of the Kingdom of God.[9] He instructed the Church to proclaim the good news of a kingdom.[10] Before He ascended, Jesus taught for forty days on the Kingdom.[11] Jesus began and ended with the subject of the Kingdom. He described His message as *"good news of the kingdom."* This is not peripheral to the gospel. If we understand the gospel, it will keep us from falling prey to nationalism, but the fact most Christians do not know what the "Gospel of the Kingdom"[12] is reveals we have lost sight of something fundamental to our message.

The gospel is the good news that God is forming a nation under His Son Jesus. Any time we confuse this Kingdom with the nations of this age, we distort the gospel and inevitably cause confusion and great harm. We should serve our nations, be model citizens, and celebrate our cultural distinctions, but there is only one Nation that will remain in the age to come: *the Church.* We are a part of this Nation now, and it is our primary nationality. Many people agree with this in theory but act differently in practice.

---

[8]Matthew 4:17; Mark 1:15.

[9]Matthew 10:7; Luke 9:2; 10:9, 11.

[10]Matthew 24:14.

[11]Acts 1:3.

[12]The books *Son of Man: The Gospel of Daniel 7* and *Son of Man: The Apostles' Gospel* deal extensively with the subject of the Gospel of the Kingdom and how Jesus taught it.

There was a time in the Old Testament when the Israelites lived in Babylon as exiles. During this time of exile, Jeremiah gave specific instructions:

"Thus says the LORD of hosts, the God of Israel, to all the exiles whom I have sent into exile from Jerusalem to Babylon: Build houses and live in them; plant gardens and eat their produce. Take wives and have sons and daughters; take wives for your sons, and give your daughters in marriage, that they may bear sons and daughters; multiply there, and do not decrease. But seek the welfare of the city where I have sent you into exile, and pray to the LORD on its behalf, for in its welfare you will find your welfare." (Jeremiah 29:4–7)

The Israelites were commanded to live faithful lives, serve their families, and seek to bless their city. The Israelites did not put their hope and their future in the success and glory of Babylon. They knew they were the people of Israel and the time of exile was temporary. Even if they died in Babylon, they placed their hope in the future kingdom, not the glory of Babylon.

This is the pattern for New Testament Christianity. Like those who have gone before us, we are called to live by faith as exiles in this age, seeking the good of the cities we dwell in while living as a nation wandering among the nations of the earth:

These all died in faith, not having received the things promised, but having seen them and greeted them from afar, and having acknowledged that they were strangers and exiles on the earth. . . . But as it is, they desire a better country, that is, a heavenly one. Therefore God is not ashamed to be called their God, for he has prepared for them a city. (Hebrews 11:13, 16)

Peter described this age as our "time of exile":

And if you call on him as Father who judges impartially according to each one's deeds, conduct yourselves with fear throughout the time of your exile. (1 Peter 1:17)

He also reminded the saints that we should live according to the values of our new Nation rather than the "passions of the flesh" that characterized the Roman Empire:

But you are a chosen race, a royal priesthood, a holy nation, a people for his own possession, that you may proclaim the excellencies of him who called you out of darkness into his marvelous light. Once you were not a people, but now you are God's people; once you had not received mercy, but now you have received mercy. Beloved, I urge you as sojourners and exiles to abstain from the passions of the flesh, which wage war against your soul. (1 Peter 2:9–11)

Peter urged the Church to live differently from the corrupt culture because we are "sojourners and exiles" in this age. We live among the nations, but we have no permanent home in this age. We are a nation wandering among the nations, waiting for the return of our King and the Kingdom He will establish. We are real citizens of that Kingdom now, but while we wait for His return, we live like expatriates who seek the good of the nations we currently live in.

We should live in a way that brings good to the cities we now live in with the confidence we are part of a new kingdom led by a resurrected Man. That Kingdom is real *now*, so we should not try to secure righteousness through political means or revolutions. We are part of a kingdom that has already begun and is indestructible. Nation states in this age will war against us, but this is not our war. We are part of a new kingdom, a kingdom that has come through death and resurrection.

The fact so many Christians are more emotionally troubled by political elections than the condition of their local congregations is a serious indicator we do not see the Church as our true Nation. If we put our hope in the nations of this age, we do not understand our biblical hope, we do not grasp our identity, or we have accepted an inferior substitute. We do not need to reform the nations, nor are we revolutionaries. We do not need to make the nations of this age into the "Kingdom of God." We already have a nation—an eternal, imperishable kingdom.[13] We desperately need an eternal perspective. We are already part of an everlasting kingdom. Our present and our future are connected to that Kingdom. The kingdoms of this age are momentary.

---

[13]Isaiah 9:7; Daniel 7:14, 27; Matthew 4:17; 24:14; Mark 1:15; Luke 9:1–2; 10:9, 11; Acts 1:3; 2 Corinthians 5:20; Ephesians 2:19, 6:18–20; Philippians 3:20; 1 Peter 2:9; Revelation 1:5–6; 5:9–10.

Right now, many Christians identify more with political entities than the Church, but this will change. The first-century church knew they were exiles and pilgrims, and the end-time church will know the same. In the days ahead, the Lord is going to bring shifts in the earth that cause His people to identify with their true condition. The Church is a nation *across* the nations.

The relationship between an embassy and a nation is an analogy that can help us understand the Kingdom in this age. An embassy is a miniature expression of a much greater nation. It exists in a foreign territory, but it is a genuine expression of the nation it represents. The space an embassy occupies legally belongs to the nation it represents and not the host nation. Inside an embassy, you encounter the language and culture of another nation, and obtain the permission necessary to visit the nation represented by the embassy. The embassy is not the fullness of the nation it represents, but it is an authentic expression of a nation in a foreign land.

In the same way, Jesus will establish a kingdom on earth when He returns. He is the only one who can bring the fullness of the Kingdom, but until He does, we have been commissioned to build "embassies" of the coming Kingdom called *churches*. These "embassies" demonstrate the nature and character of the Kingdom, though they are in "foreign" lands. These "embassies" are not the fullness of the Kingdom, but they are an authentic witness, and we are real citizens of the Kingdom. These "embassies" of the Kingdom invite people to join the Kingdom and take part in the coming Kingdom. Just as someone encounters the culture and government of a foreign nation when they enter an embassy, people should encounter the culture and government of the next age when they enter a church.

The Church is a present demonstration of a future reality that is coming.

A New People Group

When a person is born again, not only do they become part of a new kingdom, they also become part of a new people group. This is expressed in the New Testament as becoming a "new creation" or a "new man":

> *Therefore, if anyone is in Christ, he is a new creation. The old has passed away; behold, the new has come. (2 Corinthians 5:17)*

For neither circumcision counts for anything, nor uncircumcision, but a new creation. (Galatians 6:15)

But now in Christ Jesus you who once were far off have been brought near by the blood of Christ . . . that he might create in himself one new man in place of the two, so making peace. (Ephesians 2:13, 15)

These verses speak of much more than a spiritual renewal. Paul describes someone who is born again as a *new species* of human. When God formed born-again humanity, He formed an entirely new creation, or we could say new kind of creature. When the Holy Spirit lives inside a person, they not only become part of a new kingdom, they become part of an entirely new people group. The difference is so profound that it goes to the heart of what it means to be a human. It is a bigger distinction than race, ethnicity, gender, or any other human distinction in this age.

Anyone who is born again has become a fusion of God and man. You are no longer a "normal" human. You may look "normal" and even feel that way much of the time, but you have become an entirely different person. You are a God-infused creature, and your inner man has been radically changed.

The transformation of the new birth does not make you God, nor does it remove all the beautiful distinctions you were born with, but it makes you a new species of human. You are now like your older brother Jesus because God now dwells in your human frame.[14] The born-again reality makes you part of God's Nation. It not only gives you a new citizenship, but a new nature (species), and as a result you have more in common with another believer who cannot speak your language than you do someone who may share your passport in this age.

When we find our hope, purpose, and meaning in political entities, we do not grasp our identity as born-again humans. We are part of a new people group and in a new kingdom now, even though we live in our "old" bodies as exiles in our "old" nations. We should be connected to the hopes, desires, pains, success, and sufferings of this

---

[14]Romans 8:29.

new humanity and this new Kingdom.[15] This new creation is a kingdom and a new family. We are not family because we look the same, but because we have all been born by the same Spirit. All born-again people carry the same divine DNA in their inner man, which makes them family at a much deeper level than family in this age.

In families, people have different personalities, appearances, and opinions. People can experience deep conflict in their families, but in a healthy family, they have a deep identification with their families. They may disagree, but they defend each other's honor and have a strong sense of unity. They feel each other's pains and successes intensely. The same is true of the "new creation."

If you have more pain, fear, joy, anger, or delight in a political entity than the local church, you do not grasp your identity and are likely blinded by nationalism. If you believe God is committed to the success of certain nations and the destruction of other nations, you are also likely blinded by nationalism. If you are willing to divide the Church and break fellowship with other believers over political opinions, this is a serious sin[16] and reveals you have succumbed to the blindness of nationalism.

Nationalism in this age is the fruit of a low view of the Church.

Nationalism is fueled by pride, fear, or both. These emotions are so strong that they can lead people to do things they would not otherwise do. Both emotions are based on confidence in human strength over God's leadership. Pride is confidence in strength, and fear is confidence in weakness. Pride believes man can achieve his own destiny. This is the foundation of modern humanism and more deeply rooted in our souls than we know. Fear believes men can threaten God's purposes either by human weakness or by the triumph of wickedness. When the Church succumbs to either of these, we inevitably seek comfort, safety, and success in the wrong places, but neither emotion should drive members of the new creation.

---

[15]Isaiah 9:7; Daniel 7:14, 27; Matthew 4:17; 24:14; Mark 1:15; Luke 9:1–2; 10:9, 11; Acts 1:3; 2 Corinthians 5:17, 20; Galatians 6:15; Ephesians 2:13, 15, 19, 6:18–20; Philippians 3:20; 1 Peter 2:9; Revelation 1:5–6; 5:9–10.

[16]1 Corinthians 1:10; 11:18; 12:25; Philippians 1:27; 1 Thessalonians 5:13; 1 Peter 3:8.

Avoiding Political Prostitution

The book of Ezekiel details God's indictments against His people. He used very direct language and, at times, used allegories to show how he felt about His people's sin. Two of the most graphic indictments are found in Ezekiel 16 and 23. In these chapters, God accused His people of the worst kinds of covenant unfaithfulness. He described Israel as His wife, but a wife who was not just adulterous but a "brazen prostitute":

> *How sick is your heart, declares the Lord GOD, because you did all these things, the deeds of a brazen prostitute. (Ezekiel 16:30)*

Both chapters detail Israel's sin against God through this lens of adultery and prostitution. The actual sin was very simple: Israel tried to secure the promises of God through political means. Instead of remaining loyal to YHWH, Israel sought her blessing, security, future, and the promises God had given through political means. She acted politically and sought alliances to secure her future. It looked wise, and the people assumed God would bless it, but God saw it as prostitution.

Not surprisingly, this still occurs in our day. Widespread democracy has made this even more acceptable because we act as though the future of the nations is determined by human decisions and democratic processes. We lack confidence in God's assertion that He leads history for His purposes, even if humans resist Him. We do not have to seek political power or try to use nations to achieve an outcome we think God wants or to obtain a blessing God has promised.

We should be good citizens and speak up about issues of righteousness when we have the ability to petition our governments, but the political structures of this age cannot secure our promises. God alone will fulfill the promises He has spoken to us. We must be at rest in His good sovereignty. If we have more raw emotions about elections than we do our local church, it is a sign Ezekiel's rebuke could apply to us.

OUR RESPONSIBILITY TO THE NATIONS IN THIS AGE

It is imperative that we relate properly to nations in this age. With this in mind, we can summarize our relationship with the nations as follows:

- We are to be witnesses of another age and another kingdom. We cannot expect fully righteous government in this age.

- We are to honor, respect, and submit to government leaders—even wicked ones—as authorities under God's sovereignty. We are messengers of the Kingdom of God, not political revolutionaries. The Bible exhorts us to obey authority, not seek to overturn it.

- We should pray and work for the peace and prosperity of the nations we live in.

- It is misleading to give people the hope of a "righteous nation" in this age because it is an unbiblical hope. When people continue to advance the cause of a "Christian nation," it produces several issues. First, it divides the hope of the Church between this age and the age to come. Our ultimate hope is not in this age but in the age to come. Second, it causes people to put a disproportionate effort, driven by fear or hope, in political attempts to "establish the Kingdom" instead of putting their primary effort in building the Church. Third, people become disillusioned when things they hoped for do not come to pass.

- We should be faithful witnesses of the truth. This means we speak plainly according to what the Scripture says about issues of righteousness, injustice, etc.

- We should work tirelessly for the Church to be a demonstration of a just, loving, holy, and righteous people. God wants to show His goodness and nature to the Church through His people. Far too many Christians have prioritized political work over building the Church. We need to shift this focus back to the Church.

- We recognize the gospel is the solution to man's dilemma. Political and social actions can be helpful, but they cannot address man's root issue. Unjust laws can (and should) be changed, but laws cannot change the human heart.

- Verses that describe the nations at the end of the age do not describe any nations in positive terms. All have profound, underlying issues.

The New Testament apostles lived in a politically complex world filled with injustice and nationalism, and yet we find no political commentary in the New Testament. Instead, they focused on building the Church and the people of God becoming a mature, holy people who lived according to the pattern of Jesus. Some believe the New Testament pattern does not apply to us because we live in a different time with greater ability to influence government. We should use the opportunity to influence government for good, but we must remain true to the foundations laid for us. We expand the gospel by building the Church, not by seeking political influence or objectives.

Just because many of us can vote in elections does not mean we should relate to government differently from the way the apostles did. We must not abandon the framework given to us by the apostles.

When we put more emphasis in political action than building the Church, it exposes our humanism. We think we can accomplish God's purposes through human structures, but it will not work. The Church is the only structure God has given us to accomplish His purposes.

We must remember there is a difference between *functional* superiority and superior *righteousness*. There are systems of government and economics that are functionally superior to others because they provide increased opportunity. However, functional superiority does not mean a superior righteousness. It is possible to be a prosperous nation with excellent human rights and not be righteous. If you are given political influence, you should use that to seek the good of your nation, but these benefits cannot produce biblical righteousness.

Some governments seek to maximize human freedom. Freedom and human rights can produce much good, but when maximum freedom exists, the ability to pursue all sorts of evil exists as well. The heart is not cured of sin by freedom. Other governments establish more controls on human behavior. These controls can limit human sin, but they cannot reform the human heart. Furthermore, there is a constant temptation to use control for personal benefit. Nations are forced to choose an imperfect path between the two extremes. Some systems are superior to others in the way they function, but none can produce a truly righteous people. None can transform the heart. Even modern forms of democracy can perpetuate injustice and be guilty of horrible acts.

Some put their trust in the freedom of the individual, and others put their confidence in the wisdom of many. Some look to capitalism, others look to socialism, and most look to hybrid systems. While a system may function well, no system is the one "biblical" system. They are all imperfect, human systems that are not capable of a biblical righteousness. If we expect the systems of this age to produce righteousness, the Lord will eventually expose our assumptions because no nation can bear that weight, not even nations that some believe are "Christian."

We should be grieved by wickedness in society but not in despair. We should speak up for righteousness and vote when given the opportunity, but the hope of a righteous government in this age is not a biblical hope. Like Daniel, we should work for good wherever the Lord places us. We should not be passive, but neither should we hope for something the Bible does not promise.

The Lord did not tell us to try to disciple nations in this age. God may put people in political places for His purposes, but He advances His purposes through His people throughout society. No one job is more important than another. Wherever we are, we should be an influence for good and faithful in our vocations.

We have learned from Job, Habakkuk, Isaiah, and Jeremiah, but there is one more prophet we need to consider—a man who demonstrated what God wants from us.

THE BIBLICAL PROTOTYPE OF THE MATURE CHURCH

The little book of Daniel is much more significant than it appears at first glance. The entire book is a prophetic message, and to recognize that message, you must understand the role of Daniel in the book. Daniel is very unusual because he is flawless in the book. He shows no weakness and makes no mistakes. It is extremely unusual for an individual to be presented this way in the Bible. Daniel is presented this way because, in the context of his book, he represents something. He is a prototype.

Daniel lived through a prototype of the end times. Nebuchadnezzar was an antichrist figure. He was proud and arrogant. He commanded people to worship a statue at the point of death. He destroyed Jerusalem and took the Jews as slaves. This historical story is a prototype of something the Bible says will come at the end of the age.

Joseph is one of the premier prototypes of Jesus in the Bible, and Daniel is often considered a Joseph figure because there are several similarities. For example, both were carried away as slaves, both served gentile kings, both interpreted dreams, both suffered unjustly, and both ended up in a prominent position. However, Daniel is also different from Joseph. Joseph had power and authority that Daniel never had. Daniel exerted authority through obedience, faithfulness, endurance, and intercession.

Joseph and Daniel have differences because Joseph is a prototype of Jesus, but Daniel is a prototype of the mature end-time church.

In his book, Daniel consistently faced the tests that the end-time church will face, and he passed them all. For example, Daniel lived through an antichrist figure, great compromise, suffering, and the seduction of Babylon. God strengthened him with supernatural revelation and insight. In fact, Daniel could be the best prototype of the mature Church in the Bible.

Daniel is a picture of the mature Church who will overcome the core human issue we have exposed through the lives of Habakkuk and Job.

Daniel's Simple Secret

Daniel's secret is revealed in the first chapter of his book. The book begins during a prototype of the end-time crisis. The wicked and arrogant King Nebuchadnezzar had begun a series of military invasions that destroyed Jerusalem, demolished YHWH's temple, and carried most of the people from Judah into exile. Daniel 1 tells Daniel's story of being carried away in captivity. He was taken from his family, likely made a eunuch, and forced into the king's service.

In Daniel's time, people assumed that each nation had a national god. As a result, Babylon's victory over Judah was assumed to be the victory of Babylon's god Marduk over Judah's God YHWH. An ancient person would have seen Nebuchadnezzar's victory as a sign YHWH was unable to preserve His people, His temple, or fulfill His promises. When Daniel arrived in Babylon, the city was glorious and the people were confident. The Jews were humiliated and YHWH seemed unable to protect them. When Daniel was put in the king's service, everything he had experienced and seen indicated the promises of God had failed.

Daniel faced Eve's test. Would he trust what he could perceive and what he experienced or what God said?

Daniel's secret was simple: Daniel put more confidence in the Word of God than what he saw and experienced. He chose to be loyal to YHWH when YHWH seemed to have failed. He suffered because it seemed YHWH's promises had failed, and yet he remained faithful to promises that seemed impossible. He persisted through several tests and the rule of several pagan kings. He served Babylon and then Persia with excellence. Both pagan empires oppressed his people, but Daniel believed God was sovereign over pagan empires, so he served these empires in excellence rather than pursuing revolution against them.

Daniel had a political position, but he did not seek Israel's future through political means; he prayed. Daniel's confidence in YHWH enabled him to serve in the halls of a foreign government with excellence, and his life reveals the biblical path for those who find themselves working in governments. He embraced where the Lord had placed him and did his work with great skill even though he served empires who persecuted his people.[1]

Daniel prayed the promises of God with fasting, mourning, and repentance.[2] When he was told God's promises would come long after he was dead, he continued to fast, mourn, and pray for those promises.[3] Daniel endured incredible tests and trials. Not only could he not see God's promises, he suffered tremendously. He lost his family. He was carried away as a slave. He lived his life in a foreign land under the constant pressure of the Babylonian and Persian systems. As an old man, he was thrown to lions. He never returned to his homeland, and he did not see God fulfill the promises he longed for. However, over decades, he had more confidence in what God had said than what he saw, observed, and experienced.

Daniel did not always understand what God was doing, and many of his visions confused him, but he persisted in his trust. Because of this, he became a primary prototype of the mature Church, and he was told by Gabriel he was "greatly loved" by God.[4]

The mature end-time church will pass through life and the end of the age with the confidence of Daniel. Even if every human sense provides "evidence" God has failed, the mature Bride will trust Him absolutely. Even unto death.

---

[1] Daniel 1:19; 2:48; 6:3.

[2] Daniel 9:1–4.

[3] Daniel 10:1–3.

[4] Daniel 9:23; 10:11, 19.

PRAYING RIGHTLY

Intercession is one of the primary ways we partner with God to advance His activity. As we discovered, Habakkuk was a frustrated intercessor, and many intercessors in the Church are as well. The way we pray exposes our deepest dreams and fears. As Jesus said, what comes out of man reveals what is in his heart.[1]

Some of our frustrations are legitimate expressions of grief, but others flow from wrong assumptions about God's leadership:

- We assume God needs to "intervene" which is not true. He is deeply involved.

- We assume He only leads us to blessing and prosperity, but this is not true. The New Testament predicts the opposite. It predicts suffering will be a challenge until Jesus returns, and it never promises prosperity in this age.[2]

- We assume God is interested in our success in this age, but He is not. He is interested in our maturity and committed to our eternal success, which is very different from our fortunes in this age.

- We assume we can fully anticipate what God will do and grasp the logic of His leadership. In reality, we do not have the capacity to understand His ways.

---

[1]Matthew 15:19–20; Mark 7:21–23.

[2]Matthew 16:21, 24; 24:9; Mark 8:31, 34; Luke 9:22–23; 24:26, 46; Acts 5:40–41; 9:16; 14:22; Romans 5:3–5; 8:17–18; 2 Corinthians 4:17–18; 11:23; Philippians 1:29; 3:10–11; 2 Thessalonians 1:5, 9–10; 2 Timothy 2:10–12; Hebrews 2:10; 5:8; 10:32–37; 1 Peter 1:3–7, 11; 2:19–21; 4:13–14, 19; 5:9–10; Revelation 2:10.

- We assume men govern the nations through democracy or brute force unless God "intervenes," but this is not true.

- We assume that God is committed to our nationalistic hopes and dreams, but He is not.

- We assume He is untouched by our suffering, when He has suffered far more than any other person.

- We assume we are alone in our suffering, but we are not.

When we allow these assumptions to infect our thinking, it affects our ability to pray. As Habakkuk discovered, God is so kind that He responds to our intercession even when we do not know what He is doing. However, He has given us a way to avoid Habakkuk's crisis and stay in line with His will. It is profoundly simple: *We must pray Bible verses.*

The Bible contains the words of God, and this gives us perfect language for conversation with Him. If we pray the Bible, we know we are praying in agreement with God, and this practice will renew our minds so we can think like Him. When we pray the Bible, we may not know *how* God will do what He has promised to do, but we can be sure He will do what He has committed to do.

Intercession with Assumptions

Praying the Bible will help us let go of the assumptions that accompany our prayers. For example, when we pray for revival, many of us assume that churches will be full and the economy will be strong. Consider the shocking testimony of a pastor in a war-torn nation where Christians experienced severe persecution. I remember his solemn words as he shared, "We prayed for revival for years, and it has come, but we never thought it would come like this." The revival they longed for had come in the middle of an incredible crisis.

This does not mean revival is always accompanied by economic or political upheaval, but it may come differently than we expect. God may advance His work through a time of peace and prosperity as He did in the first century when a peace known as the "Pax Romana" (Roman Peace) allowed the gospel to spread quickly, or He may use an escalating crisis to answer our prayers. We usually associate the "kindness" of God with our continued comfort, but God may disrupt our comfort in His kindness. If a disruption causes millions of men and women to face the real questions about their own eternity and seek salvation, then the disruption is a profound kindness. Discomfort for a few years in this age cannot compare to everlasting salvation.

God always acts with eternity in view. Our horizon is simply too short.

God is not unmoved by wickedness in the nations. He does not overlook sin. He will judge wickedness, but He has not surrendered His sovereignty. Even when evil seems to prevail, God's purposes will be accomplished. Therefore, no matter how dark it seems, we can pray with confidence.

God may use disruptions, but we should still pray for mercy. Mercy is our great need, and God loves to give it. He may or may not give His mercy in the ways we expect, but we must pray for it. He will release mercy in partnership with human intercessors.[3]

God's sovereignty should not lead us to be fatalistic; it should cause us to engage with more tenacity. God *is* active. God *does* answer prayer. As Habakkuk discovered, He still acts in response to our intercession even when we do not grasp what He is doing.

We have favor with God because of what Jesus did, not because of our maturity. We should pursue maturity, but prayer does not need to be precise to be effective. Above all we need to approach God in confidence. God wants us to come *boldly* before Him knowing He hears us and we have favor with Him.[4] Maturity comes as we engage with Him and allow Him to change us. Habakkuk's prayers were not precise, but his pursuit of the Lord created the context for his blindness to be removed. If he had not engaged the Lord in intercession he would have remained blind. *We must avoid passivity.*

If God rebukes us, we must remember that His rebukes are an expression of His desire. They flow from His heart of love.

---

[3]For more on this, see my book *Mercy Before Judgment.*

[4]Ephesians 3:12; Hebrews 4:16; 10:19–23.

CHRISTIANITY IS REVEALED NOT DISCOVERED

Christianity is a revealed religion not a discovered one.

When we gaze at the person of Jesus, we can trust God's character absolutely, though we cannot fully anticipate His ways. God's wisdom cannot be fully seen until *after* He acts. The majesty of His leadership is often only visible in hindsight. This was true in the crucifixion of Jesus, and it will be true again at the end of the age.

The root of all sin is the desire to evaluate God. Generations have put God in the court of history and rendered our verdicts on the smallest details of our lives and the biggest calamities. The vast majority of Christians assume they agree with God's ways, but in reality they agree with what seems reasonable to them. Even theologians can be caught in this trap, trying to interpret passages in ways that make them reasonable to "modern human ethics" rather than letting God speak for Himself and being willing to confront our own assumptions.

Most of the Church has not yet been tested like Job and Daniel. If that day comes, will we agree with God when He seems completely "unreasonable" to us?

The Enlightenment has influenced nearly every part of our world. It took the sin of the garden and developed an entire system of thought around it. God was essentially exiled to the world of "religion," and we developed systems of science, government, ethics, and education that assume man can discern what is best on his own and does not need input from God. The Enlightenment rejected divine revelation and embraced the sin of the garden openly as the path of salvation for mankind. From the beginning, it was a direct challenge to the God of the Bible, and it cannot win that challenge.

The philosophy that developed from of the Enlightenment is so pervasive that it feels normal and reasonable to us. We hardly question it, but the Bible presents a radically different philosophy that confronts the faulty human premise that man can evaluate good and evil and secure his future by reason. God is going to confront and expose this faulty foundation, but first He wants to address it in the Church.

We now have enough history to see the futility of human wisdom. Century after century, we see that man's wisdom cannot solve his core issues. Yet, we continue to prefer our own wisdom over God's, thus continually demonstrating the sin of the garden remains alive in our hearts. For example, the twentieth century saw some of the greatest advancements in human history but also brought two world wars and terrifying implements of war.

Like Habakkuk, we continue to hold God up to our system of ethics instead of learning His ethics. While this seems reasonable, especially to Western thinkers, it is setting us up for failure. God will not remain under our examination; He is the one who evaluates us. Our evaluation of His activity—even His judgments—does not matter.[1] He does not answer to us; we answer to Him. No matter what we think, we will ultimately appear before *His* judgment seat. He will not stand before ours.

God is not content with the development of a "Judeo-Christian" system of ethics which fuses Western thought and human wisdom with some biblical principles. We must return to the deep conviction that "good" is defined by God Himself. Whatever He does is *good*. If we want to know good, it is not ultimately defined by moral codes—it is defined by a Person.

We should defend the faith and graciously present the reasonable basis for Christianity. However, Christianity is not ultimately built on reasonable assumptions. It is based on the revelation of God. The apostle Paul was one of the most brilliant men in history, and he was not converted by a better argument; he was converted by revelation. Not everyone will have that same experience, but the principle is the same. Human wisdom cannot lead us to the truth. God must reveal the beauty of His Son.

---

[1] Isaiah 40:13–18, 25, 27; 1 Corinthians 2:16.

God Is Not Discovered, He Is Revealed

It is time to reform our thinking and recover the God-centered paradigm of reality that Job, Habakkuk, Isaiah, and Daniel were confronted with. This comes by revelation from the Spirit, not from human reason. The human mind cannot discover the ways of God because it is at war with the knowledge of God:

> *For the mind that is set on the flesh is hostile to God, for it does not submit to God's law; indeed, it cannot. (Romans 8:7)*

We must resist the temptation to create explanations for things that offend or confuse us. Instead, we need to learn to sit silently before Him and allow Him to renew our thinking and liberate us from humanistic thinking that taints our minds and even hides in our seminaries. If you want the knowledge of God, you must let God reveal Himself and must endure the pain and the tension of that revelation when it violates your understanding of reality, what is reasonable, and even what seems right.

Truth is not a set of ideas we can discover. It is defined by a Person. Truth is whatever He is. Therefore, you must allow Him to define reality rather than trust in your own senses. Whatever He reveals about Himself is true regardless of whether you can comprehend it or agree with it.

When people are shocked by God, they have one of four responses: They are offended and reject Him; they avoid things they cannot understand; they create explanations for what God said that ultimately redefine what He has plainly revealed about Himself; or they allow God to transform their thinking.

If you have been shocked by God's revelation of Himself, do not relieve the shock prematurely. Do not run to commentaries searching for rational explanations; bear the tension and wrestle with what God has said about Himself and about His people. If you want to see reality the way it really is, you have to allow God to deconstruct your faulty paradigms.

If you prematurely relieve the tension between what He says and what you assume is right, you will miss something valuable. If you stay in the tension and allow Him to deconstruct your thinking, you will end up with a renewed mind and begin to discover the vast ocean of the knowledge of God. You must be willing to let go of your human thinking if you want the knowledge of God. You must be willing to allow God to reshape your mind, and this means being willing to deny your own wisdom and even your own grasp of reality.

If you want to know God, you must seek Him in the way He reveals Himself. Because we cannot discover Him by reason alone, the Holy Spirit reveals God to us in a number of ways. Not only can we hear His voice, He also communicates to us in a number of ways that reveal God. Above all He gives us spiritual insight into the Person of Jesus who is the ultimate revelation of God. The Spirit also speaks to us through the Scripture. He also speaks through other believers, and we typically experience the ministry of the Spirit through the Body. In fact, the people of God are the primary evidence of Jesus in this age.[2]

Tragically many people think of the revelation of God as a private, individual experience, but God reveals Himself in and through His corporate Body. While we must all have a personal revelation of God, God has made this age an immersive classroom and He reveals Himself to us through His people.

We must embrace the ways God reveals Himself to us, and there are three in particular we must eagerly pursue: communion with the Holy Spirit, the written Scripture, and life in the Church with the Body of Jesus. As we engage in these three elements we will discover the revelation of God and be kept from deception and unbiblical ideas. The first two in particular must be pursued individually *and* in spiritual community. If you pursue a life of private devotion but neglect the corporate ministry of the Holy Spirit, the Word, and the gifts He distributes throughout the Body, you will lack aspects of the revelation of God.[3]

God will not speak to you individually about everything you need for maturity because He is not looking for people who are self-sufficient. In many cases, you will hear the voice of God from others in the Body. Paul reminded the Corinthians that "we" have the mind of Christ.[4] Paul used a collective rather than individual word as a reminder that God's thinking is found in fellowship His people.

---

[2] John 17:21, 23.

[3] 1 Corinthians 12; 14:1–18.

[4] 1 Corinthians 2:16.

You Must Begin with God

If you want to know God, you must begin with God. We struggle to grasp God because we do not begin with God. We think we do, but in reality we try to comprehend God with preconceived ideas about reality, time, morality, ethics, and ourselves. The only answer to this is to allow God to reveal Himself.

We live in an age that assumes human potential is unlimited, but the first step to the knowledge of God is acknowledging our limited capacity and being willing to submit to His revelation of Himself even when it does not make sense. Modern thinking is man-centric. This way of thinking is so pervasive the gospel is often thought of and communicated in a man-centric way that begins with the needs of man instead of the revelation of the glory of God.

We cannot truly think biblically if we begin with the power of human critical thinking, because reality is not built around man, it is built around God. It's time to turn out the lights on the Enlightenment and recover a biblical paradigm of reality.

The God Who Defines History

It is time to recover our confidence in God's leadership of history. We should not overlook or excuse evil. However, the fate of history is not in human hands nor in the hands of spiritual powers. It is firmly in the hands of the one who made it all. Many Christians are confident God was involved in the past, and many expect God to be actively involved in the "end times." But God is just as active in history now as He has ever been.

God's people often see His work in hindsight while struggling to see it in their own generation. We often miss His work because of assumptions that blind us and because we fail to see His hand in our ordinary, daily lives. However, He is just as present in the ordinary parts of life as He is in the "crisis." We forget that Jesus lived 90 percent of His life in obscurity in a small village doing the normal tasks of first-century life.

He is present. He is sovereign.

Many have settled for an individualistic Christianity where God is the Savior of people's "souls" but not really intricately involved in history. This is not an accurate portrait of the God of the Bible. He transforms individuals, but He also leads history. Day by day, we grow more confident in human achievement and human potential. However, that confidence will end in a massive disappointment in a future day when God will be seen in His majesty again. This day will be stunning, offensive, overwhelming, and majestic. The prophets struggled to describe it. He will show Himself again in a "second exodus"[5] far beyond the ancient exodus and lead history into the age to come.

This is our hope.

We must learn the lessons of the prophets, particularly their lessons in crisis and disruption. These stories were written to *prepare* us, not just *inform* us. Many of the prophets lived through incredibly disruptive times, but the Lord described His ancient activity as "silence" compared to what He will do in the end:

> For a long time I have held my peace; I have kept still and restrained myself; now I will cry out like a woman in labor; I will gasp and pant. (Isaiah 42:14)

Jesus repeatedly declared His identity as Judge and predicted He will judge.[6] He is both Savior *and* Judge. He is the same one who judged in the Old Testament. His words to the prophets about His judgments are designed to prepare us for a greater day of judgment coming. The idea that God judged in the Old Testament but no longer judges is patently false. It is a perversion of the New Testament gospel. Consider just a few verses:

> "The times of ignorance God overlooked, but now he commands all people everywhere to repent, because he has fixed a day on which he will judge the world in righteousness by a man whom he has appointed; and of this he has given assurance to all by raising him from the dead." (Acts 17:30–31)

> Since indeed God considers it just to repay with affliction those who afflict you, and to grant relief to you who are afflicted as well as to us, when the

---

[5]Exodus 34:10; Deuteronomy 30:1–10; Isaiah 4:5; 11:11–16; 64:1–3; Jeremiah 3:16–17; 16:14–15; 23:7–8; 30:8–10; Joel 3; Habakkuk 3:3–15; Micah 7:15–17; Zechariah 10:8–9; 14.

[6]Matthew 9:6; 10:15, 32; 11:22, 24; 12:27, 36, 41–42; 13:41; 16:27; 19:28; 25:31–32; Mark 8:38; Luke 9:26; 10:14; 11:31–32; 12:8–9; 18:8; 21:36; John 3:18–19; 5:22, 24, 27, 29–30; 8:16; 9:39; 12:31, 48; 16:8, 11.

Lord Jesus is revealed from heaven with his mighty angels in flaming fire, inflicting vengeance on those who do not know God and on those who do not obey the gospel of our Lord Jesus. They will suffer the punishment of eternal destruction, away from the presence of the Lord and from the glory of his might. (2 Thessalonians 1:6–9)

But by the same word the heavens and earth that now exist are stored up for fire, being kept until the day of judgment and destruction of the ungodly. (2 Peter 3:7)

While we wait for that day, we live in absolute confidence in His leadership. Leading families well. Discipling others. Blessing our neighbors. Knowing whatever trials we pass through will produce profound good in our lives if we cooperate with Him because no one can thwart His purposes or comprehend His ways.

He is not safe—but He is good.[7]

When You See, You Will Worship

When God reveals Himself, there is only one response: *worship*.

When we encounter Him, we instinctively respond with worship. Just as a crowd erupts in praise when they see a tremendous feat and humans are awed by the majestic power of a storm, the heart will erupt in praise when it sees the majesty of God.

Habakkuk was never given a reason for God's leadership, but his book ends with singing. He sang in absolute confidence in who God is. He sang of God's salvation, even if he did not see it in his lifetime:

Though the fig tree should not blossom, nor fruit be on the vines, the produce of the olive fail and the fields yield no food, the flock be cut off from the fold and there be no herd in the stalls, yet I will rejoice in the LORD; I will take joy in the God of my salvation. (Habakkuk 3:17–18)

Habakkuk could sing because he had encountered God and had absolute confidence in God's goodness. Just as a small child trusts a good father, Habakkuk could trust God in matters he could not understand because he had confidence in God's person and His ultimate goodness.

---

[7]C.S. Lewis, *The Chronicles of Narnia* (New York, NY: Harper Collins, 1982), 146.

God's sovereignty over all history is both controversial *and* immensely comforting. Evil did its worst in the crucifixion of Jesus, and in that act, evil suffered its greatest defeat. If this was true for Jesus, it is true for God's people as well.

We do not need better "answers"; we need a deeper revelation of God. This revelation is found in the person of Jesus and perhaps most of all in His suffering. He alone can resolve our unanswered questions and our hidden fears. He does not resolve them by giving us an answer we can evaluate—He resolves them with Himself.

Habakkuk, Job, Isaiah, Jeremiah, Daniel, and many others never fully understood what God was doing, and God did not answer all their questions. However, they "saw" God, and their confidence in Him answered every accusation in their hearts. Their stories have been written for our sake to give us profound confidence in the daily perplexities of our lives, the crisis moments of our lives, and especially if we live through a great time of crisis.

Now is the time to pursue this knowledge of God. So many are offended now, and our crises are relatively small. Let's pursue the knowledge of God *now* in all our little disappointments and all the unexpected twists and turns of life.

We do not need better and more logical answers; we need a better revelation of the majesty of God in the Person of Jesus.

Author Bio

Samuel Whitefield's primary labor is as an intercessor in the context of night-and-day prayer. He is the director of OneKing, a ministry that helps connect the global church to God's purposes for Israel and the nations. He also serves as faculty at the International House of Prayer University. His passion is to declare the beauty of Jesus until He is loved and adored on earth as He is in heaven (Matthew 6:10; Revelation 5:13).

For additional resources, please visit samuelwhitefield.com.

ACKNOWLEDGMENTS

Thank you to my wife whose labor and sacrifice make it possible for us to engage in the task the Lord has given us.

Thank you to the entire family for enduring the process that has produced the message in this book.

Thank you to Stuart Greaves for your friendship. Your insight into Habakkuk and your commitment to the text has provoked me and played a significant role in my own journey with Habakkuk.

Thank you to Jeffery Jackson for your encouragement, your friendship, and your investment in this project. I am grateful for you.

Thank you to Edie Mourey for your work on this manuscript.

Thank you to the prayer team who has faithfully prayed for this book. The Lord released grace in response to your petitions.

Printed in Great Britain
by Amazon

62622892R00129